Cambridge Elements ≡

Elements in Metaphysics
edited by
Tuomas E. Tahko
University of Bristol

PROPERTIES

Anna-Sofia Maurin
University of Gothenburg

CAMBRIDGE
UNIVERSITY PRESS

CAMBRIDGE
UNIVERSITY PRESS

University Printing House, Cambridge CB2 8BS, United Kingdom

One Liberty Plaza, 20th Floor, New York, NY 10006, USA

477 Williamstown Road, Port Melbourne, VIC 3207, Australia

314–321, 3rd Floor, Plot 3, Splendor Forum, Jasola District Centre, New Delhi – 110025, India

103 Penang Road, #05–06/07, Visioncrest Commercial, Singapore 238467

Cambridge University Press is part of the University of Cambridge.

It furthers the University's mission by disseminating knowledge in the pursuit of education, learning, and research at the highest international levels of excellence.

www.cambridge.org
Information on this title: www.cambridge.org/9781009009249
DOI: 10.1017/9781009008938

First published 2022

A catalogue record for this publication is available from the British Library.

ISBN 978-1-009-00924-9 Paperback
ISSN 2633-9862 (online)
ISSN 2633-9854 (print)

Properties

Elements in Metaphysics

DOI: 10.1017/9781009008938
First published online: July 2022

Anna-Sofia Maurin
University of Gothenburg

Author for correspondence: Anna-Sofia Maurin, anna-sofia.maurin@gu.se

Abstract: Although the subject matter of this Element is properties, do not expect in-depth introductions to the various views on properties "on the market." Instead, here that subject matter is treated *meta*-philosophically. Rather than ask and try to answer a question like *do properties exist?* this Element asks what reasons one might have for thinking that properties exist (what problem properties, if they exist, are there to solve), what counts as solving that (or those) problem(s) (including what counts as "a property"), as well as how we ought to proceed when trying to find out if properties exist (by which method this ought to be decided). As it turns out, these questions and their answers are all intricately intertwined. Theory comparison and evaluation is, in other words (and perhaps not that surprisingly), tricky. Do properties exist? After reading this Element all we can say is therefore this: that depends.

Keywords: properties, metaphysics, meta-philosophy, theory-comparison, theory-choice

ISBNs: 9781009009249 (PB), 9781009008938 (OC)
ISSNs: 2633-9862 (online), 2633-9854 (print)

Contents

Preface

Take a walk around town. Observe the houses, the people, the litter. Appreciate the cut of one woman's coat. That woman's coat is olive green. Note that olive green seems to be particularly popular this fall. Sit down at a café and order a cup of coffee and a cinnamon bun. "That's one enormous bun," you think to yourself. "It's so heavy!" Worry a bit about saving room for dinner, then pull out pen and paper to write down your experiences. "There were houses, people, and lots of litter," you write. "I liked the cut (but not the color) of one woman's coat." "Olive green seems to be especially popular right now." "I prefer forest green to the color of that woman's coat." Finish your bun. You're golden.

Apart from obvious life lessons such as that forest green is the superior color or that you can never go wrong if you opt for a cinnamon bun, here's another thing we can learn from reflecting on your morning walk: some things appear to exist (at least we talk as if they do), play a role in reasoning, are foundational to our categorizing behavior, yet do not – at least not at first glance – qualify as what we call "objects" (whatever objects may be). These things include but are by no means limited to things like shapes (the cut of that woman's coat), colors (olive and forest green), and weights (such as that of the cinnamon bun you just devoured). These things are commonly called *properties*, and they are the topic of this Element.

Philosophers have been debating the nature and existence of properties since the birth of philosophy itself. Not surprisingly, then, there now exists a plethora of different theories on whether properties exist, on what properties are like (if they exist), as well as on how we ought to proceed when answering questions about the existence and nature of properties in the first place. A common way to approach the topic of properties is via an in-depth introduction to the several (primarily realist) theories on (the nature of) properties people have at some point in history found it worthwhile defending, followed by an introduction to the various challenges these accounts must face and how they could face them, followed by a discussion of which of these theories – if any – we ought to prefer and why. Recent – really good! – introductions to the topic along these lines include Edwards (2014) and Allen (2016).[1]

This Element approaches its topic in a slightly different way. Rather than provide in-depth introductions to the various views on properties "on the market," it takes much of that kind of knowledge for granted. The focus is instead on the following questions: (1) What is/are the problem(s) of properties? (2) Given a particular understanding of the problem(s) of properties, what

---

[1] Another really good "warm-up" text is McDaniel (2020: chapter 2).

method should we use to tackle them? (3) What difference – if any – does what you happen to identify as *the* problem of properties, as well as what you happen to identify as *the* method for solving that problem, make to how you answer the question *do properties exist?*

1 Introduction

Perhaps not surprisingly, just because philosophers have been debating the existence and nature of properties since the dawn of time, it doesn't follow that the theories people have proposed and defended can be straightforwardly evaluated and compared, or that it is even clear *what* those theories are theories of, or, indeed, whether what those are theories of is always the same thing. To illustrate, consider the distinction between *property realists* and *property nominalists*. In the literature this distinction is commonplace. Yet, although most of us involved in this debate think we understand it, saying exactly what it is that the realist and nominalist disagree about is surprisingly tricky.

Here's one – common – way to answer that question: what realists and nominalists disagree about is whether reality contains only particulars, or if it contains both particulars and universals (Armstrong 1978a: 1). If you regard the disagreement between realists and nominalists as one concerning the existence or not of *properties*, this way of characterizing what is at stake is problematic, however. For, arguably, being a universal is not the only way to be a property (cf. Maurin 2019). In any case, insisting that it is, is to rule – without argument – that, for example, trope theory (a view traditionally introduced as saying that there are properties, yet properties are particular) is a view on which *properties don't exist.*[2]

To avoid this consequence, one might try a more direct route and say that what property realists and property nominalists disagree about is whether reality contains entities belonging to the category *property*. At first glance, this would seem to cut the cake the right way. Those who hold views typically categorized as "realist" – classic examples include Platonism, immanent realism, and (I will from now on assume) trope theory – all agree that there is a category – *property* – to which some entities that exist belong. Likewise, those who defend views typically categorized as types of "nominalism" – for example, mereological-,

---

[2] Other reasons to be skeptical of equating "being a universal" with "being a property" include: (1) the fact that it is not even clear what "being a universal" amounts to (cf., e.g., Ehring (2011: part 1.1) and Giberman (fc.)), and (2) the fact that, if we regard universals as entities able to exist fully "in" distinct objects at one and the same time – which is a common view – Platonic Forms (which exist apart from the objects that exemplify or partake in them) are not really universals. If this makes Platonism a kind of nominalism, it seems we are left with an understanding of the distinction too far removed from how it is normally taken to make much sense.

class-, resemblance-, and ostrich nominalism – all agree that there is no such category or, at least, that there is nothing belonging to that category.[3, 4]

But what does to accept (or to reject) the existence of entities belonging to the category *property* entail more precisely? As we shall see in a moment, philosophical debate about the existence and nature of properties is often understood in linguistic terms as concerning which existence and/or existence-presupposing claims we ought to regard as true and meaningful, or as concerning whether certain terms in our language (e.g., predicates and/or nominalizations) refer. This circumstance might make one think that what accepting (or rejecting) the existence of entities belonging to the category *property* amounts to can be put in terms of which sentences one takes to be true and which false: that a property realist is someone who thinks that sentences like "properties exist" or "there's a property of that woman's coat that I like very much" are (possibly) true, and that a nominalist is someone who takes them to be (always) false. However, if this is what realists and nominalists disagree about, we're now forced to categorize as realist views normally considered as types of nominalism.

To see this, note that if what the conflict between nominalists and realists boils down to is what truth-value we think certain sentences (ostensibly about properties) have, then only the rather few philosophers who are eliminativists and/or error-theorists about properties and property-talk would count as "true"' nominalists.[5] Most of the aforementioned (traditional) nominalists are, however, neither eliminativists nor error-theorists. Although they reject the existence of properties, they mostly don't reject *the truth* (or meaningfulness) of sentences ostensibly about properties. Some of them don't even reject the referentiality of (at least some) "property terms," but rather claim that those terms refer to something – in reality – *that is not a property* (like, e.g., a resemblance-class of objects). Should all those who reject the error-theoretic approach to property-talk count as realists about properties? To answer this question with a "yes, they should" is to hold an unusual and probably rather controversial view. Still, if accepting or rejecting the existence of entities

---

[3] For advanced introductions to these various realist and nominalist views, cf. (on Platonic Forms) Balaguer (2016), (on trope theory) Maurin (2018), (on nominalism) Rodriguez-Pereyra (2019), and (on properties generally) Orilia and Paolini Paoletti (2020).

[4] That those who tend to be called nominalists hold that nothing belongs to the category property is only half true. Lewis (1983) categorizes classes – however miscellaneous and gerrymandered – of objects as *properties*. Rodriguez-Pereyra (2002) sometimes does the same for his resemblance-classes of objects, which is yet more proof of how conceptually confusing this debate has become.

[5] To error-theorists about properties (cf., e.g., Båve 2015), the raison d'être of words like "property" is to increase the expressive power of languages in which they figure, yet because sentences including words like "property" should be taken at face value and so interpreted literally, those sentences are all false.

belonging to the category *property* is understood simply in terms of which sentences we take to be true and meaningful, it is an answer we thereby accept.

What, then, is the difference between those who think property-talk is true and meaningful, that at least some terms ostensibly about properties refer, yet that *there are no properties* and those who on the basis of the same or similar sorts of considerations about language, meaning, and reference conclude that *properties exist*? The answer may seem obvious: the difference lies in *what* more precisely it is they think must exist in order for their statements – including statements like "properties exist" – to be true.

What thing is that? This is something about which reasonable people disagree. According to the Platonist, first, when a property exists, something abstract and transcendent, necessarily existent (but only contingently exemplified, if exemplified at all), exists. According to the immanent realist, on the other hand, properties (must) exist in the objects they characterize and can exist in more than one place in space at one moment in time. According to the trope theorist, when a property exists, an abstract particular exists in the object that exemplifies it.[6] To say of two objects that they "share" a property is, on this view, to say that they each contain a trope such that those tropes belong to the same (resemblance-)class. And according to some so-called nominalists, finally, what exists when it seems as if properties exist, or when we talk as if properties exist are certain types of (abstract) sets or classes of objects, either primitively individuated or formed on the basis of the resemblance of their members.[7]

(Resemblance-)classes of objects are both different and distinct from, for example, Platonic Forms, immanent universals, or tropes. But it's unclear if this fact is enough to explain why the latter types of entities are properties, yet (resemblance-)classes of objects are not. For, as we have just seen, Platonic Forms, immanent universals, and tropes are also *mutually* very different.

---

[6] To add to the confusion, note that "abstract" means different things on these different views. To a Platonist it means (among other things) "non-spatiotemporal." But this cannot be what the trope theorist means (as her posits exist *in* space-time). For more on what "being abstract" has been taken to mean, see Section 3.3.2.

[7] An influential proponent of the Platonic view is (surprise, surprise!) Plato (cf., e.g., the *Republic*). A version of immanent realism is often said to have been defended by Aristotle (cf., e.g., his *Categories* and *Metaphysics*). The most influential contemporary immanent realist is D. M. Armstrong (cf. esp. his 1978a, 1978b, and 1989). One of the earliest trope theorists was D. C. Williams (cf. his collected works, published 2018), cf. also Campbell 1990, Maurin 2002, and Ehring 2011). Among the nominalist positions mentioned earlier, resemblance-class nominalism is probably the one most discussed in the literature (cf., e.g., Rodriguez-Pereyra [2002] for an influential defense). Not mentioned is so-called ostrich nominalism. This view is not mentioned here because it is a view on which statements that seemingly pick out properties don't even pick out something playing the property role (not even classes of objects, that is). This view will be further discussed in Section 3.

Moreover, Platonic Forms, immanent universals, tropes *and* (resemblance-) classes of objects play a similar (at least an overlapping) role: they are what exists when properties seem to exist; they are what we refer to when it seems as if we refer to properties. But then, at least on some views normally categorized as types of "nominalism," there are entities that do not belong to the category *property* but are nevertheless able to play the property-role (i.e., the role realists claim only *properties* can play). Which prompts the question: if not with reference to the role those things can or cannot play, how are we to distinguish (real) properties from their non-property stand-ins?

Perhaps the issue – if it's even worth calling an issue – is merely verbal. I'm fine with that verdict. The problem is that because talk of "realism" and "nominalism," about what exists and what doesn't, about what is true and what is false, about what refers and what doesn't, has become so well entrenched in our theorizing about properties, and because, in so theorizing we have, consciously or not, started to think about such talk as clustering in certain ways (realism, exists, true, and refers go together, and so do nominalism, doesn't exist, is false, doesn't refer), a merely verbal confusion risks leading to a substantial one.

The moral is this: to be able to evaluate and compare different views on the nature and existence of properties, we must first understand what those theories are theories *of* as well as *how* those theories are justified and why. Because these things are not always explicit, the risk that theory evaluation and comparison is question-begging or at least a little bit confused is high. This Element is an attempt to minimize this risk by focusing precisely on and making explicit the different methodological and other assumptions on which theorizing about properties can be said to rest. In Section 2 this is achieved through a study of some prominent ways of understanding *the problem* of properties. The following two sections, Sections 3 and 4, constitute the bulk of this text. Here two different approaches to *how* one ought to determine whether properties exist are critically investigated. Section 3 first investigates the idea that whether properties exist is something to be decided through a close study of language only. Section 4 next investigates alternative – nonlinguistic or not-entirely-linguistic – approaches to the problem of properties. Section 5 finally contains a brief summary and conclusion.

2 The Problem

For a piece of metaphysics to count as *a theory*, whether or not it includes entities belonging to this or that category must always be motivated. Typically, you motivate adding a kind of entity to your ontology by pointing to some perceived theoretical need: the theory must include entities belonging to kind Φ because Φ:s are needed to account for Ψ, where Ψ is some phenomenon we deem problematic or at least in need of an explanation. This type of reasoning is characteristic also of theorizing about properties. Those who think there are properties motivate their introduction with reference to one or several "need(s)" that they think only properties can fill (or at least that they think properties can fill the best). Those who think there aren't properties, on the other hand, don't think this is a need that only properties can fill or that only properties can fill well, or they think that the need identified by the property realist isn't really a need in the first place and so filling it is not required.

In this section we investigate the idea that the need properties are there to fill is the need to explain or in some other way account for (instances of) a special kind of fact: the fact of the One over Many. That properties *can* fill this need is accepted by most. This means that, when philosophers disagree about the existence of properties, what they disagree about is most likely not that. Rather, what they disagree about is if properties not only can but must be posited to fill this need. Or what they disagree about is if it is *this* need, and not some other(s) filling of which will decide if properties exist. (How) can these disagreements be (dis)solved? As I will try to demonstrate in what follows, to determine if only properties can account for the fact of the One over Many or if this *is* the fact that needs accounting for in the first place, we must first understand what type of fact the fact of the One over Many is.

2.1 The Fact, the Problem, and the Argument

Although so called, the problem of properties is not necessarily best conceived of as *a problem*, at least not if what you mean by that locution is something worrisome, puzzling, or otherwise incomprehensible. Rather, what most people mean when they speak of the "problem" of properties is that there is some presumably indisputable kind of fact (or, perhaps, more than one kind of fact) that whatever theory we embrace (about what there is, or, at least, about why things appear the way they do) must make room for. More precisely – since in this case the relevant problem is one *of properties* – the fact in question is at least apparently or superficially *about properties* and/or it is a fact that can be straightforwardly accounted for by a theory according to which properties exist.

Which fact is that?

Here's a type of answer that most philosophers seemingly agree on: it is the fact that distinct things sometimes appear to have something in common, or that there seem to be "ones that run through many." This is *the fact of the One over Many*, instances of which include the fact that, although both distinct and in many respects different, that woman's coat appears to have something in common with my favorite mug (color). Or the fact that the cinnamon bun I just devoured can be correctly described as having something (indeed many things) in common with this one, still displayed on the counter. And many more facts like these.[8]

Behind the idea that *the fact* of the One over Many gives rise to *a problem* lies another: that the fact of the One over Many *must be given a philosophical account*, that it *must receive a metaphysical explanation*. David Armstrong makes this point by saying that the fact of the One over Many is a "Moorean fact." The idea is then that Moorean facts are like the commonsense facts mentioned by Moore (1925). They are what, for example, Goldstein (1983: 40) calls "trivial observations," or what Legg refers to as "incontrovertible claim[s]" (Legg 2001: 117). According to Armstrong (1980: 442, emphasis added):

> [T]he fact of sameness of type is a Moorean fact: one of the many facts which even philosophers should not deny, whatever philosophical account or ana-lysis they give of such facts. Any comprehensive philosophy must try to give some account of Moorean facts. *They constitute the compulsory questions in the philosophical examination paper.*

Facts that we on pain of irrationality understand, cannot doubt, and must accept as true – in other words, Moorean facts – are facts that must be given what Moore calls "an analysis" and what later philosophers have called "an account" or "an explanation." And *what* accounts for or (metaphysically) explains these facts is neither trivial nor incontrovertible.

That the problem of properties *is* the problem of the One over Many is an idea that can be traced back at least to Plato (cf., e.g., his *Phaedo* and *Republic*). Many of those in favor of the existence of properties – including Plato, but see also (and perhaps especially) Armstrong (1978a) – have then tied this problem to an argument: *the argument from the One over Many*. Here the idea has been that the sort of "same-ness" to which the fact of the One over Many informing the problem of the One over Many draws our attention is most straightforwardly made sense of by literally accepting that there is *one thing* – the universal – that distinct objects share. This running together of the fact, the problem, and the argument from the One over Many is found already in Plato. In, for example, the *Republic* (596b) Plato lets Socrates ask:

> Shall we proceed as usual and begin by assuming the existence of a single essential nature or Form for every set of things which we call by the same name?

Because of the strong connection (universal-)realists have tended to make between the *fact*, the *problem*, and the *argument* from the One over Many,

---

[8] The problem people derive from facts like these is sometimes – confusingly – called "the problem of universals." However, as Campbell notes (1981: 483, cf. also Oliver [1996: 47] and Rodriguez-Pereyra [2000: 256]): "the problem is not one about universals but about properties, universals being a particular solution to it."

one might get the impression that *given this fact, (universal-)realism is inevitable*. As we shall see in what follows, however, thinking this would be premature. Even if the fact of the One over Many – in appealing to "sameness" and "oneness" – on its surface seems especially suited to universal realism, that fact is better understood as neutral when it comes to which solution we ought to prefer. At least this is how I will regard it in what follows.[9]

2.2 Linguistic or Experiential

What type of fact is the fact of the One over Many? This is not always clear. In the *Phaedo* (78e; cf. also the quote from the *Republic* cited earlier), Plato – through Socrates – talks in terms that suggest that the fact in question is that there are terms in our language that can be used to describe more than one thing. This makes it sound as if instances of the fact of the One over Many are facts like this one: *that "olive green" can be truly predicated both of "that woman's coat" and of "my favorite mug."* Thus understood, instances of the fact of the One over Many are facts about language. They are linguistic facts.

Then there are other places where Plato seems considerably less inclined to identify the fact – and the problem – of the One over Many with this linguistic one, places where he seemingly prefers expressing the relevant fact instead in terms of how things *seem to him in experience* (cf., e.g., Plato's *Hippias Major*; cf. also Denkel [1996: 8ff.] for an enlightening discussion). Instances of the fact of the One over Many, then, are rather facts like this one: *that woman's coat and my favorite mug appear to have something in common; they seem to share the same color (olive green)*. This is not a fact about language. Nor is it – at least not directly – a fact about reality. It is rather a fact about how reality seems to us when we experience it. It's an experiential fact.

Plato interpretation to one side (I'll leave that to those better equipped!), what this illustrates is that we can distinguish between two types of facts of the One over Many: linguistic and experiential ones.[10] Does it matter with which of

---

[9] Although his early texts indicate that Armstrong disagrees with me, later writings reveal a much more nuanced understanding of both the fact and the problem of the One over Many, as well as of whatever argument can or cannot be derived from either. My guess is that this change is mostly due, not to a new way of understanding the fact and problem of the One over Many, but to a move toward thinking of what exists in truthmaker theoretical terms (for a sustained defense of a truthmaker-theoretical approach to metaphysics, see Armstrong [2004]). For an argument to the effect that because Armstrong is a scientific realist, the fact of the One over Many *does not* provide Armstrong with a special reason to accept the existence of universals, see Maurin (2008). For more on the truthmaker-theoretical approach to the problem of properties, see Section 4.2.1.

[10] Are there no *metaphysical* facts of the One over Many? There would be if universal realism were true. But this means that, if there are, their function is that of a *solution* to the problem of properties, not what gives rise to it in the first place.

these types of facts the fact giving rise to the problem of properties is identified? Armstrong certainly thinks so. He argues (1978a: xiii–xiv):

> [P]resenting the argument in this linguistic fashion ... encourages confusion with an unsound argument to universals from *meaning*. This ... argument moves from the existence of meaningful general words to the existence of universals which are the meanings of those words /–/ Only if we first develop a satisfactory theory of universals can we expect to develop fruitfully the further topic of the semantics of general terms.

Armstrong is here speaking of an "argument" rather than a "fact." The reason for this is that he accepts the view mentioned earlier (Section 2.1) according to which the most robust explanation of the fact of the One over Many is in terms that literally respect what that fact says: if there seem to be ones that run through many, this is because there *are* ones that run through many. Universals are by nature ones that run through many. Therefore, if there seem to be ones that run through many, universals exist. Here's the argument in Armstrong's own words (1978a: xiii):

> [The argument] is, or is a descendant of, Plato's One over Many argument. Its premiss is that many different particulars can all have what appears to be the same nature ... The conclusion of the argument is simply that in general this appearance cannot be explained away, but must be accepted. There is such a thing as identity in nature. I take this argument to be sound.

The reason why Armstrong thinks we ought to understand the fact of the One over Many as experiential rather than as linguistic is that he thinks understanding it as linguistic might make us confuse the foregoing ("sound") argument with another one – from meaning – that he believes is *not* sound: an argument according to which properties (universals) exist because they are the referents of general terms (so-called predicates). This argument takes as its point of departure the existence of true and meaningful *sentences* of the form "*a* and *b* are both F." The argument is in other words premised on the idea that the fact of the One over Many is linguistic. But if an argument premised in this way is flawed, Armstrong seems to be saying, then so is its premise.[11] Which is why we ought to regard the fact of the One over Many as experiential.

Armstrong's argument for understanding the fact of the One over Many as experiential is instructive yet ultimately flawed. Confusing a sound argument with an unsound one is of course bad, but unless we are begging the question, that confusion is possible is not in itself a reason not to regard the relevant fact as linguistic. *If* the Moorean fact of the One over Many is linguistic, and *if* the only

---

[11] Whether Armstrong really holds this view is in fact unclear. Especially in his later writings, his arguments often proceed from what seems to be linguistic rather than experiential facts of the One over Many (only then in order to provide the requisite *truthmakers* for those claims).

argumentative route available from that fact to the conclusion that properties (universals) exist is unsound, all this tells us is that the (linguistic) fact of the One over Many *does not* provide us with a reason to think that properties (in the sense of universals) exist. Indeed, it might be understood as telling us the exact opposite: that the fact of the One over Many gives us reason to think that *properties don't exist*. That (if!) this is a consequence of identifying the relevant fact as linguistic is certainly interesting. That it is, is, however, *not* a circumstance that counts against so identifying it.

Armstrong hence fails to demonstrate that we *ought to* identify the fact of the One over Many with the experiential one, but he succeeds in demonstrating (perhaps unconsciously) that *how* we identify the relevant fact might turn out to have rather substantial consequences. If Armstrong is right, which fact is *the* fact of the One over Many may matter to which problem (of properties) can be formulated on its grounds, which may matter to what methods can or should be used to solve that problem, which may matter to what conclusion – concerning the existence or not of properties – using those methods will compel us to draw. If you like, the following two sections can be seen as an illustration of this.

3 Going Linguistic

As I use this terminology in what follows, to "go linguistic" means two things. First, it means taking as your primary explanandum the linguistic fact of the One over Many. Second, it means accepting that whether properties exist is something you decide through a close study of language *only*.

That both of these things are required for an account to count as "going linguistic" is important to keep in mind. Quite a few philosophers accept the linguistic fact of the One over Many as their primary explanandum yet do not accept that whether properties exist is something you can decide using only linguistic means. Most of these philosophers are truthmaker theorists and so think that properties, if they exist, are there to make true propositions. Because they accept only one of the requirements for "going linguistic," these philosophers and their philosophies of properties are *not* the topic of this section (but are the topic of Section 4).

Another group of philosophers who it may seem as if they should count as "going linguistic" but whose views I will disregard in what follows are the so-called (neo)Carnapians (cf., e.g., Price 2009 and Thomasson 2015). The (neo)Carnapians take all truths to be true *relative to a linguistic framework*. In this, they (not surprisingly, perhaps) take their cue from Carnap. According to Carnap, it is *because* all truths are true relative to a linguistic framework that:

> ... the alleged questions and answers occurring in the traditional nominalism-realism controversy, concerning the ontological reality of universals or any other kind of entities, [are] pseudo-questions and pseudo-statements devoid of cognitive meaning. (1947/1956: 43).

According to Carnap, although we cannot ask (and answer) questions about the – external – reality of, for example, properties, we *can* ask (and answer) "internal" questions. Asking an internal question about properties amounts to asking if properties are anything this or that linguistic framework says there is. But asking (and answering) *this* question is not very interesting. For, according to the (neo)Carnapian, given a linguistic framework featuring a true subject-predicate statement, *that* properties (internally) exist is easily (some would say trivially) demonstrated using what Schiffer (2003) calls "something-from-nothing-transformations" (cf., e.g., Section 3.3, but note that there the transformation is used to make a decidedly non-(neo)Carnapian point).

Is there anything real or substantial left for (neo)Carnapian realists and nominalists to disagree about? Yes. But what remains to disagree about does not concern *what there is*. It concerns if we, for pragmatic reasons, ought to prefer a linguistic framework with predicates and/or nouns seemingly referring to properties, or if we should go for one that features none of those terms instead.

It is of course important to be aware of the (neo)Carnapian view, if for no other reason than to be able to correctly interpret claims about the existence or not of properties by philosophers belonging to this camp. For the purposes of this Element the (neo)Carnapian view will, however, be ignored. When the realist and the nominalist disagree about the existence of properties we simply assume that they are having a *substantial* disagreement in the sense that what they disagree about is *what there is* (either because they believe that you *can* ask and answer external as well as internal questions, or because they refuse to acknowledge that distinction in the first place).

How can I justify making this assumption? Well, for one, it is an assumption made by most of those involved in debates over the nature and existence of properties (including those whose views are the topic of this section). Pointing this out is of course not the same as justifying the assumption made. When it comes to the "deeper" question of which view on the nature of existence, ontology, the relationship between language and reality, and so forth one ought to prefer, I half suspect that whatever argument I present in favor of regarding metaphysical debates as substantive will not be accepted by those who prefer the opposite view. And vice versa. This is because those who reject and those who accept the (neo)-Carnapian approach to ontology understand the project they're involved in *very* differently. Perhaps the difference is so great as to make the two approaches incomparable. I'm not sure. In any case, this is where I leave that question.[12]

3.1 From Quine to quineanism[13]

Most of those whom I count as going linguistic accept what we may call a "quinean" approach to ontology. Quine was what Armstrong (1978a: 16) called an "ostrich nominalist."[14] His was the view that:

> One many admit that there are red houses, roses, and sunsets, but deny, except as a popular and misleading manner of speaking, that they have anything in common. The words "houses," "roses," and "sunsets" denote each of sundry individual entities which are houses and roses and sunsets, and the word "red" or "red object" denotes each of sundry individual entities which are red houses, red roses, red sunsets; but there is not, in addition, any entity whatever, individual or otherwise, which is named by the word "redness," nor, for that matter, by the word "household," "rosehood," "sunsethood." That the houses and roses and sunsets are all of them red may be taken as ultimate. (Quine 1948: 29–30)

According to Quine, in other words, "*a* and *b* are both F" can be both true and meaningful, yet there need be nothing the predicate – F – in that statement picks out. That *a* and *b*, which exist, are both F "may be taken as ultimate."

The reason Quine doesn't think accounting for the truth and meaningfulness of the (linguistic) facts of the One over Many requires positing the existence of properties is that Quine, not surprisingly, is a quinean. According to the quinean, what exists is what the true sentences of our "best theory" *ontologically commit* us to. Finding out what those commitments are, moreover, involves more than simply gauging what those sentences – on their surface – *seem* to ontologically commit us to. To illustrate, consider the following (true) statement:

(1) that woman's coat is olive green

---

12 For a recent critique of the (neo)Carnapian approach from the point of view of a devoted quinean, cf. van Inwagen 2020.

13 Throughout this Element I opt for denoting views similar to or derived from those of Quine using lowercase "q." I'm fully aware that this is unusual. I do this because, although they methodologically overlap, the "quinean" approach to ontology most likely differs significantly from that imagined by Quine himself (cf., e.g., Section 3.3 for an example of this). The lowercase "q" is there to make sure that this is *very* clear.

14 This term was introduced by Armstrong as a somewhat derogatory label for the view. According to Armstrong, in defending his brand of nominalism, Quine is like an ostrich hiding its head in the sand, refusing to answer a compulsory question (cf. Section 4.1.1 for a discussion of this claim). A less derogatory label is "austere nominalism." Since "ostrich nominalism" is now a well-established name for the view, used not just by its detractors but also by its proponents (cf., e.g., Imaguire 2014 and Guillon 2021), I will, however, stick to it in what follows.

On a traditional view of language, meaning is compositional (cf. Szabó 2020), from which it follows that the meaning of (1) is the product of the meaning of its parts such that, once the meaning of those parts has been fixed, the meaning of the whole is fully determined. On a traditional view of language, moreover (1) is a subject-predicate sentence. As such it has two parts: a subject – "that woman's coat" – and a predicate – "is olive green." Given compositionality, the meaning of (1) is hence the product of the meaning of those parts. And on a traditional view of language the meaning of "is olive green" is a property (or a "concept"). Which might make one think that, in order to account for the meaningfulness of sentences like (1), we must accept that *properties exist.*

Of course the meaning of (1) is the product of the meaning of its subject and predicate parts, only if those *are* the meaning-bearing parts of that sentence. However, according to the quinean, they aren't. Rather, (1) – indeed, *every* sentence seemingly of subject-predicate form – is *really* an existential generalization. (1') makes this explicit:

(1') *There exists something* that is a coat owned by that woman and that is olive green.

Why think that *this* and not the subject-predicate form is the "real" form of this type of sentence? Because of a riddle Quine dubs "Plato's beard." This is "the old Platonic riddle of non-being," which arises given the (seeming) fact that, in order to say of something that it does not exist, "[n]on-being must in some sense be" (Quine 1948: 21; cf. also Russell 1905). To illustrate, consider the following well-known example:

(2) Pegasus does not exist

Suppose we treat the surface-form of (2) as if it were its real form. Then (2) is a subject-predicate sentence. Because we know that Pegasus is a mythical, made-up animal, we know that (2) is true. And if (2) is true, it must be meaningful. As we have seen, given compositionality, a sentence has meaning in virtue of the meaning of its sub-sentential parts. Hence "Pegasus" has meaning. What meaning is that? "Pegasus" is a proper name, and proper names are normally taken to mean their reference. Therefore, if "Pegasus" has meaning this is because there is something to which that name refers. Given that we – along with Russell and Quine and certainly many more – refuse to accept that something that does not exist (but nevertheless "has being," cf., e.g., Reicher 2019) can serve as the referent of anything, it follows that, in order for (2) to have meaning, what "Pegasus" refers to must *exist*. But then what (2) ontologically commits us to is whatever "Pegasus" names, and what (2) says is that whatever "Pegasus" names (which exists) *does not exist*. Plato's beard, it turns out, is tangled.

One way to untangle Plato's beard would be to simply reject the traditional view of language and compositionality just set out. Suppose we're unwilling to do that. Then quineanism is the way to go. To see this, note that the source of the problem is that, if (2) is a subject-predicate sentence, then – given compositionality – its subject term must have a meaning that, given a common view of the meaning of proper names, is its reference. What the quinean proposes is, however, that sentences like (2) *are not* subject-predicate sentences. According to the quinean, to find out what form a sentence has (any sentence, not just problematic sentences like [2]), it is hence not enough to superficially inspect it. The "true" logical form of a sentence is the form revealed once that sentence has been translated into (first-order predicate) logic. What a sentence ontologically commits us to – what exists – is then what the bound variables of that sentence range over. To the quinean, in other words, to find out what a sentence like (2) ontologically commits us to, we must first transform (2) in a way that brings its true form to the surface. Doing so will reveal that sentences like (2) are existential generalizations. Thus understood, what (2) says is *not*, paradoxically, that *there is something that does not exist*, but rather that:

(2') *there is nothing* such that that thing is Pegasus[15]

If Plato's beard gives us reason to accept quineanism, what can quineanism tell us about the existence of properties? As we have seen, Quine himself was a staunch nominalist. At least prima facie it is easy to understand why. If what our sentences ontologically commit us to is what those sentences' bound variables range over, what (1) ontologically commits us to – what exists – is *that woman's coat* (a fact made explicit in [1']). In general, what laying bare the underlying logical form of a statement like "*a* is F" reveals is that what that statement says is that *there exists something* that is F and that is identical with *a*; "*a*" (in this case "that woman's coat") is a singular term (or a definite description behaving like a singular term), and what singular terms normally pick out are (ordinary) objects. But then sentences like (1), if true, do not commit us to

---

[15] Throughout this Element I have opted for *not* expressing myself using symbolic logic. This means that, as in the case of (1') and (2'), "translations" of sentences into first- (or second-) order predicate-logical form are expressed using natural language. For the most part I think this way of doing things should be pretty straightforward. In some cases there may be room for misunderstanding, however. Given some comments I've received, (2') might be a case in point. So, just to be clear, I'll make an exception. What (2') says, more precisely, is that: $\neg(\exists x)((x{=}a)$ and $((\forall y)((y{=}a) \supset (y{=}x))))$.

anything besides "sundry individuals," which means that accepting quineanism gives us reason to accept nominalism as well.[16]

Quineanism does not *entail* nominalism, however. One reason it doesn't is that sometimes a sentence like "*a* is F" will feature a so-called nominalization in the subject position.[17] Here's one example:

(3) humility is a virtue

A nominalization is a noun (a subject term) created from an adjective or a verb (a predicate). Intuitively, nominalizations *do not* pick out objects. Rather, nominalizations appear to pick out properties. (3) has the same superficial form as do (1) and (2) and so the result of transforming it into first-order predicate logical form ought to be the same: a sentence which bound variables range over whatever that sentence's subject term seemingly picks out. If "*a*" in "*a* is F" is a nominalization and if nominalizations typically pick out properties, therefore, what a sentence like (3) ontologically commits us to is a property.

This may make it sound as if quineanism rather entails that properties *exist*. As we see in Section 3.3, however, since the quinean accepts that we can always try paraphrasing away (apparent) reference to properties, it most likely doesn't.

3.2 From quineanism to Ostrich Nominalism

As we have seen, given quineanism, simple subject-predicate statements – statements of the form "*a* is F" – do not ontologically commit us to properties (at least so long as the subject term isn't a nominalization). But what can this tell us about whether properties are needed to solve *the problem of properties*? That problem, remember, is generated from the One over Many, which, given that we are here going linguistic, is the problem of accounting for or metaphysically explaining the truth and meaningfulness of statements of the following form: "*a* and *b* have the same property, F-ness," "*a* and *b* are both F."[18]

---

[16] At this point you may wonder why understanding (1) as (1') liberates one from positing something to which the predicate refers. After all, even if understanding what appears to be a subject-predicate sentence as an existential generalization means that, for example, definite descriptions and/or names "disappear" in the final analysis, the same is not true of the predicates. The short answer is that if what exists is what we must quantify over, and if (1') does not quantify over predicates (or what predicates pick out), (1') does not commit us to properties. As we shall see (esp. in Section 3.4.1), this is, however, not an answer without (possibly serious) problems. For now I ask you to accept it.

[17] For more reasons not to think quineanism entails nominalism, cf., for example, Sections 3.3 and 3.4.

[18] So far in this text I have alternated between speaking of "statements" and of "sentences" while clearly intending by those different locutions more or less the same thing. You may or may not have a problem with this. Devitt (whose views are the topic of this section) throughout talks of "statements." Others seemingly prefer "sentence." Here I simply assume that "statement" and "sentence" can be used interchangeably while letting this footnote signal that I'm aware that

To see why one might think that a quinean analysis of simple subject-predicate sentences contributes to a solution to the problem of properties, we need to consider a now classic paper by Michael Devitt (2010).[19] In this paper Devitt argues – against Armstrong – that it would be wrong to think that the fact of the One over Many (in invoking "shared" properties, sameness of type, etc.) gives us any special reason to think that properties, especially properties understood as universals, exist. Devitt's argument for this conclusion takes as its point of departure precisely the sort of statement we previously identified with the linguistic fact of the One over Many:

(4) *a* and *b* have the same property, F-ness

Those realistically inclined would probably point out that a statement like (4), among other things, ontologically commits us to the existence of *something* that *a* and *b* share. However, Devitt is a quinean and so doesn't think that a statement need carry its ontological commitments on its sleeve: if what we are interested in is what (4) ontologically commits us to, we must first make those commitments more transparent by paraphrasing (4) as:

(5) *a* and *b* are both F

But (5), Devitt points out, is just a (thinly disguised) conjunction. What (5) says is, in other words, that "*a* is F and *b* is F," a statement that can be broken down into its two constituents:

(6) *a* is F

(7) *b* is F

And now we can see that the fact of the One over Many has disappeared. For neither (6) nor (7) say anything whatsoever about "sharing" of properties or sameness of nature. Those are rather simple predications, which means that, if there is any problem of properties left, it is the problem of accounting for or explaining the truth and meaningfulness of *those* statements. And, as we have seen, given quineanism, *this* "problem" is easily solved: "*a* is F" is true if and only if there exists an *x* such that "*a*" designates *x* and "F" applies to *x*. "There is no refusal here 'to take predicates with any ontological seriousness,'" says Devitt. And he continues:

---

things may be more complicated than that. For a nice discussion (and criticism) of reading too much into the difference between "statement" and "sentence," cf., for example, Quine 1953 (esp. pp. 440f.).

[19] Devitt's paper was originally published in 1980. The 2010 reference is to a collection of papers by Devitt. The paper can also be found in Mellor and Oliver (1997: 93–100).

> The [q]uinean thinks that there *really must exist something* (said as firmly as you like) that the predicate "F" applies to. However that thing is not a universal but simply an object. Further, in denying that this object need have properties, the [q]uinean is not denying that it *really* is F (or G, or whatever). He is not claiming that it is "a bare particular." He sees no need to play that game. (2010: 16)

Has Devitt succeeded in (dis)solving the problem of properties and has he (thereby) succeeded in rejecting property realism? Only provided that we accept, not just that ontology is best done linguistically, or that the way to "go linguistic" is to "go quinean," but also provided that we accept a couple of further assumptions about the nature and function of language. The rest of this section consists in a critical investigation of at least a subset of these further assumptions. As I try to demonstrate in what follows, these are all assumptions over which reasonable quineans may disagree. Which is bad news for the quinean. For, as I also argue, this is a sign that the quinean may not be equipped to answer the question "do properties exist?" after all. At least it is a sign that he may not be equipped to answer that question in a non-question-begging way.

3.3 Paraphrase

Paraphrasing is central to quineanism and, not least, to quinean nominalism. First, because to hold that subject-predicate sentences are "really" existential generalizations *is* to accept that sentences of the former type can be transformed or *paraphrased* into sentences of the latter. Second, because for Devitt to be able to conclude that the proper explanandum – the sort of statement we "owe" an explanation of – is *not* the (linguistic) fact of the One over Many but another (also linguistic) fact – "*a* is F" – he must first convince us that (4) can be paraphrased as (5).

If our end goal is to show, not just that the problem of the One over Many can be (dis)solved, but that there is no other – at least no other *linguistic* – need, filling of which requires properties, moreover, paraphrase is instrumental in yet another way: to take care of the special class of (from the point of view of the nominalist) problematic statements in which not the predicate but the subject term seemingly names not an object but a property.[20] Here's one by now familiar example:

(3) humility is a virtue.

---

[20] As Moltmann (2004: 1) notes: "In the context of natural language, therefore, properties apparently can act not only as possible meanings of predicates, but also as genuine objects, namely when they are referred to by a nominalization of a predicate."

Given quineanism, paraphrasing (3) into an existential generalization reveals that what that statement ontologically commits us to is humility. Humility, most would agree, is a property. Therefore, what sentences like (3) ontologically commit us to is the existence of properties. To the nominalist this is an unhappy result. To avoid it what is needed is, again, recourse to the right paraphrases. More precisely, what the quinean with a taste for desert landscapes must do is *first* paraphrase (3) into a sentence that does not feature terms seemingly referring to properties in the subject position, and *then* paraphrase the results of her first paraphrasing efforts in a way that reveals their "underlying" logical form. So, for instance, could the quinean nominalist propose we paraphrase (3) as:

(3') humble people are virtuous people

... a statement he would then transform in a way that reveals its underlying logical form, a form that does not ontologically commit him to anything but "sundry individuals" or, in this case, "sundry individual persons."[21]

Given how central paraphrasing is to the quinean project, therefore, it would be good to know exactly what paraphrasing *does*. Prima facie the answer is straightforward: what paraphrasing does is make more transparent the *real* or *fundamental* ontological commitments of our statements. Unfortunately (for the quinean), what this answer entails more precisely is considerably less clear. In Sections 3.3.1 and 3.3.2 I discuss why that is.

3.3.1 Hermeneutic or Revolutionary?

If what paraphrasing does is make more transparent our real or fundamental ontological commitments, does it follow that, if Φ is a paraphrase of Ψ, then whatever Φ ontologically commits us to *is what there is*? Not necessarily. This is because saying of paraphrases that they make more transparent our real or fundamental ontological commitments is compatible with either of two really rather different views on what paraphrasing *is* (cf. Rosen and Burgess 2007).

According to the first, paraphrasing is "revolutionary." This is the view on paraphrasing Quine defends. In, for example, *Word and Object* he states that:

> Synonymy, for sentences generally, is not a notion that we can readily make adequate sense of; and even if it were, it would be out of place in these cases. If we paraphrase a sentence to resolve ambiguity, what we seek is not

---

[21] As it happens, since (3') may be false even though (3) is true, (3') is by most *not* regarded as a good enough paraphrase of (3). The literature is full of ingenious attempts to provide adequate paraphrases for sentences like (3) that do not have this problem. Managing this for *every* sentence of this kind is, however, probably impossible.

a synonymous sentence, but one that is more informative *by dint of resisting some alternative interpretations.* (1960: 159, emphasis added)

And then, again:

[T]here is no call to think of [a paraphrase] as synonymous with [the original]. Its relation to [the original] is just that the particular business that the speaker was on that occasion trying to get on with, with the help of [the original] among other things, can be managed well enough to suit him by using [the paraphrase] instead. (160)

If Φ is a revolutionary paraphrase of Ψ, Φ and Ψ are not synonymous; they do not mean the same thing. This means that Φ does not express what Ψ "really" means. Rather, if Φ is a revolutionary paraphrase of Ψ, Φ and Ψ are both distinct and different and the "job" of the former is to replace the latter *because it more transparently reports what the speaker wants to convey.*

Thus understood, it does not seem as if paraphrasing has a role to play in ontological theorizing, linguistically understood.[22] The reason why not is simple. Revolutionary paraphrases are there to reveal what we (already) believe. But if paraphrases are simply tools with the help of which we make clear which kinds of entities we accept and which we like to avoid (even find offensive), then paraphrases *report* rather than *justify* those preferences. If, for example, you prefer desert landscapes and I do not, then, given the revolutionary approach to paraphrase, my paraphrase of "*a* and *b* are both F" as "there is a property, F-ness, that *a* and *b* share" and your paraphrase going in the other direction, so long as they successfully report each of our respective ontological beliefs, are equally "correct."

The alternative is to view paraphrase as "hermeneutic." On this view, if Φ is a hermeneutic paraphrase of Ψ, Φ and Ψ must be synonymous; they must mean the same thing. What paraphrasing does, on this view, is *reveal* what the original sentence says there is by replacing it with another one that wears its ontological commitments on its sleeve. *Pace* the revolutionist, the hermeneutic hence does not view the function of paraphrase as that of reporting our ontological beliefs, but as *revealing* what must exist in order for certain statements to be true. From the point of view of regarding paraphrasing as a tool for drawing ontological conclusions, this approach holds considerably more promise. All well? Not really. For, as we shall see next, the hermeneutic paraphraser must face the so-called problem of symmetry, a problem serious enough to threaten the whole enterprise of arguing either for or against the existence of properties from language.

---

[22] Hence the lowercase "q" in "quinean"!

3.3.2 The Problem of Symmetry

The problem of symmetry (cf., e.g., Keller 2017; for a classic formulation of this problem cf. Alston 1958) is a problem exclusively for those who accept the hermeneutic approach to paraphrase. If Φ is a hermeneutic paraphrase of Ψ, Φ and Ψ are synonymous. If Φ is a revolutionary paraphrase of Ψ, they are not. Synonymy is a symmetrical relation – if Φ means Ψ, then Ψ means Φ. If Φ is a hermeneutical paraphrase of Ψ, therefore, Φ and Ψ must be symmetrically related. Not so if paraphrasing is revolutionary.

The *problem* of symmetry is this: if the relationship between Φ and Ψ is symmetrical, on what grounds can we say of either of two statements that one is more ontologically perspicuous than the other (Oliver 1996; Mellor and Oliver 1997)?

Solving this problem is important. To see this, consider an example inspired by the sort of "easy" argument proposed by the (neo)Carnapian (whose views I briefly discussed in the introduction to this section), in favor of the existence of properties. According to the (neo)Carnapian, the existence of properties can be derived from innocent-sounding truths like (1), using so-called something-from-nothing transformations like this one:[23]

   (i)   that woman's coat is olive green
   (ii)   that woman's coat has the property of being olive green
   (iii)   there is a property that woman's coat has: being olive green
   (iv)   there are properties

Why bring this up here? The reason is that, although this is most likely not how it was originally intended, the (neo)Carnapian argument for the existence of properties can be given a quinean spin: it can be read as an argument in favor of a particular view on *what there is*. How? By being interpreted as an argument taking us from the ordinary subject-predicate statement (i) – via paraphrase – to (ii), and then from (ii) to a statement making explicit that what (i) (and [ii]) ontologically commit us to are properties.[24]

What is the difference between a quinean argument taking us from ordinary subject-predicate truths to the conclusion that properties don't exist and this one? Both accept (some version of) (i) and (ii).[25] And both view one of these

---

[23] Cf. Hofweber 2016. Chapter 2 of that book is an especially helpful resource if you want to understand what's going on in these types of arguments.

[24] To work, this argument in its quinean interpretation may also require that we translate our statements into second-order rather than first-order logic. For more on our choice of logics, cf. Section 3.4.2.

[25] "A version" because, as we have seen, the quinean normally starts with some version of the (linguistic) One over Many – "*a* and *b* are both F" – which is then treated as a disguised conjunction of "*a* is F" and "*b* is F," respectively.

statements as a paraphrase of the other. The difference lies in which statement they regard as paraphrase and which as paraphrasee. The ostrich, first, *starts* with a version of the "quinean realist's" (ii). This, he claims, is a statement that can be more transparently put in terms of (i), a statement which true logical form reveals its ontological commitments (which, as it happens, do not include properties). The quinean realist, on the other hand, starts with (i), which she holds is more transparently put in terms of (ii), which is then further transformed into (iii), a statement according to which *properties exist*.

Some philosophers have criticized this transformation for being invalid.[26] Why? Because they think (ii) is only a (more revealing) counterpart of (i) *if properties exist*. The argument is invalid, in other words, because it involves a *petitio principii*. If this is right, it should not make the ostrich nominalist feel his must be the superior view, however. For it is difficult to see why the same objection could not be wielded also against him. Ostrich nominalists – *just like* quinean realists – accept that (i) and (ii) are each other's counterparts, that they are synonymous. If it follows from this that (ii) is a more fundamental counterpart of (i) only *given that properties exist*, it should also follow that (i) is a more fundamental counterpart of (ii) only *given that they don't*. Precisely *because* they are symmetrically related, it seems we cannot – in a non-question-begging, nonarbitrary way – distinguish between paraphrase and paraphrasee. But if we cannot, how can we know – on quinean grounds – whether properties exist?

Here's one suggestion: we can always tell paraphrase and paraphrasee apart because *paraphrasing is in the direction from less to more ontologically parsimonious*. In other words, even if Φ and Ψ are synonymous, if Φ ontologically commits us to fewer (types of) entities, Φ is a paraphrase of Ψ, not the other way around.[27]

Accepting this view means accepting something like Ockham's razor – that is, it means accepting a principle of parsimony urging us not to posit (kinds of) entities *beyond necessity*. Something like Ockham's razor is accepted by most, which should make this a prima facie reasonable – perhaps even attractive – option. But is it helpful? Can urging that we paraphrase in the direction of more ontological parsimony help us decide which of, for example, ostrich nominalism and quinean realism ought to be accepted? At first glance, it may seem as if it can. If ostrich nominalism is true, only objects exist. If quinean realism is true,

---

[26] Cf., for example, Field 1984 and Yablo 2000. Cf. also the discussion in Hofweber 2016: 22.

[27] How can Φ and Ψ mean the same thing yet entail different ontological commitments? The short answer is that they cannot. The long answer is that they can. At least they can if what you mean by that is that, if the ontological commitments translating Φ directly into first-order predicate logic reveal are fewer than the commitments translating Ψ into first-order predicate logic reveal, Φ is the more ontologically revealing of the two (and hence Φ is what Ψ "really" means, not the other way around).

there are properties. Ostrich nominalism is more ontologically parsimonious than quinean realism. Therefore, *properties don't exist.*

Not so fast. A theory according to which properties exist is not automatically less parsimonious than one according to which they don't. For one, according to a non-negligible number of property realists, not only do properties exist, *there is nothing but properties.*[28] On this view, then, when it *seems* as if our statements ontologically commit us to objects, the original statements can always (at least in principle) be replaced with statements that refer to nothing but (bundles of) properties.[29] Leaving to one side if the requisite paraphrases can in fact be produced, *if they could* it seems a principle of ontological parsimony lacks the force to adjudicate between a view on which (only) objects exist and one on which (only) properties exist.[30]

Here's another suggestion: we can always tell paraphrase and paraphrasee apart because *paraphrasing is in the direction from more to less ontologically contentious.* In other words, even if Φ and Ψ are synonymous, if Φ ontologically commits us to ontologically speaking less objectionable (types of) entities, Φ is a paraphrase of Ψ, not the other way around.

Suppose – with most philosophers – that objects are reasonably unobjectionable entities. Then, if we have reason to think that properties are not unobjectionable or are *more* objectionable than are objects, we have reason to suppose paraphrasing in the direction of statements according to which properties don't exist should always be preferred to going in the other direction. Do we have reason to suppose that

---

[28] Cf. also Pickel and Mantegani (2012), who argue that *even if* we understand the property realist as someone who accepts the existence of *both* properties and objects, her view will still turn out to be more parsimonious than that of the ostrich nominalist.

[29] Objection: the bundle view presupposes *more* than just the bundled properties; it presupposes some sort of bundling mechanism as well. As noted by an anonymous reviewer for this Element, this would seem to incur an ideological and perhaps also an ontological cost that might swing things in the property realist's disfavor. This is a fair point but, first, if the cost is only ideological, it is at least unclear if it is a cost that should matter to which is the more perspicuous paraphrase. Is the cost (just) ideological? Here's a reason to think so: if the bundling mechanism is to incur a further *ontological* commitment (on top of that to properties), bundling mechanisms had better be entities of another kind than properties. However, if bundling mechanisms are a kind of *relations*, and if relations are a kind of (two- or more place) *properties*, they are not. In any case (and as also noted by the same anonymous reviewer), it is not clear that the property realist *must* posit a bundling mechanism. There may be several (more or less believable) reasons why she must not: perhaps she holds a view on which, given the bundled properties, bundling is entailed (and so is a "free lunch"). Perhaps she thinks of the bundling of properties as something "brute" (cf., e.g., Markosian 1998). Perhaps, finally, she believes that, although there are properties that exist when certain statements are true, there are no *bundles* of properties (i.e., because some sort of ontological nihilism is true, cf., e.g., O'Leary-Hawthorne and Cortens 1995). And so forth.

[30] In Putnam's words: "Sometimes we have the choice of either doing without one batch of entities, call them the A entities, or doing without another batch, call them the B entities – the reduction may be possible in either direction. In such a case, Occam's Razor [the principle of parsimony] doesn't know who to shave!" (1987: 76).

properties – but not objects – are an objectionable kind of entity? According to a pretty large majority of the nominalistically inclined quineans, we do; properties – but not objects – are objectionable because properties – but not objects – are *abstract*, and "being abstract" is an objectionable kind of feature. Quinean realism is a view on which properties exist. Ostrich nominalism is a view on which they don't. Ostrich nominalism is therefore less ontologically contentious than is quinean realism. Therefore *properties don't exist.*

Again this is too quick. To be abstract is compatible with "being" in many different ways: "abstract" is a term that lacks a clear definition.[31] And so, by the way, is "property": as we have seen, even among those who think *properties exist*, what type of thing it is they thereby accept the existence of may vary (drastically!). Depending on what you mean by the notion, therefore, both the idea that the abstractness of properties is a point in their disfavor and the idea that properties are abstract in the first place can be rejected. But then unless we come up with some *other* reason why properties are objectionable, that paraphrasing should proceed in the direction from more to less objectionable is not a reason to think that properties don't exist.

Paraphrase is central to the quinean way of doing ontology. Yet how paraphrase works – as well as if it can do whatever work it does without begging the question – remains unclear. Varzi puts this important worry very well when he points out that:

> Paraphrasability may well be a necessary condition if we want to *avoid commitment* to entities of some sort, and assertibility a sufficient condition if we want to *proclaim commitment*, but neither is necessary or sufficient to provide us with a clue to what there is. Neither is necessary or sufficient to determine the ontology itself. To put it in a slogan, linguistic analysis can be a tool for ontological investigations; but it is not a key. For the very issue of *which* sentences must be paraphrased – let alone *how* they ought to be paraphrased – can only be addressed against the background of one's own ontological inclinations. (2007: 277)

If Varzi is right, *all* paraphrasing is revolutionary. But then rather than justify our ontological commitments, what linguistic analysis can at most do is *report* what those commitments are. Which means that "going linguistic" simply cannot take us where we needed to go.

3.4 The Nature of Language

As we have seen, to go linguistic means accepting that matters to do with ontology are to be decided (at least in part) through a close study of language:

---

[31] More on this in Section 4.1.3.

given that language works *like this* we can conclude that properties exist, given that it works *like that*, we can conclude that they don't. Does language work like this or like that? This is a question on which people rationally disagree. That they do is in itself neither surprising (we're doing philosophy, after all!) nor in itself especially worrisome. At least, it should not be more worrisome than is the fact that more or less *all* theorizing departs from often contentious assumptions (which still means that it can be pretty worrisome!). Should it turn out that which account of the nature of language you prefer is at least in part decided by which ontology you prefer, things quickly start to look a lot more problematic, however: if the goal is to *reveal* what there is through a close study of language, how you understand language had better not have anything to do with which ontology you prefer!

In this section I briefly investigate two examples where how we view the nature and function of (parts of) language clearly matters to whether or not a close study of language will lead us to conclude that properties exist. As I try to demonstrate, these are also cases where it is at least unclear if how we understand the nature and function of (those pieces of) language *can be* independently justified. That is, it is unclear if this is something that can be justified on grounds that do not invoke our ontological preferences going in.

3.4.1 Predicate Reference

I start by investigating the nature and function of predicates. According to the quinean, predicates are ontologically innocent: though they contribute to the meaning of a statement by being "true of" the objects that statements' bound variables range over, they don't refer. This much is accepted even by quineans who – because they believe that some nominalizations cannot be paraphrased away – think that *properties exist*: if properties exist, it is at least *not* because predicates refer. Macbride (2006) dubs the view of the nature and function of predicates that lies behind the quinean view "disquotational" and suggests we express it schematically thus:

(P$_D$) "F" is true of x iff x is (an) F

As noted by Macbride (P$_D$) seems almost trivially true: "no-one – not even the opponents of Quine who hold that there is something more to be said about predication ... will wish to deny that the instances of [(P$_D$)] are true" (429). If (P$_D$) is accepted by both the "predicate-disquotationalist" and what we may call the "predicate-realist," what sets them apart must be something else. Let's call that something else (P$_R$). (P$_R$) is accepted by the predicate-realist, but *not* by the predicate-disquotationalist, and reads something like this:[32]

(P_R) "F" is true of x iff x instantiates the referent of "F"

If there is nothing more to the nature and function of predicates than what can be captured by (P_D), predicates give us no reason to think that properties exist. But if the nature and function of predicates is better captured by (P_R), they do. Which account should we prefer and why?

You might think that, because accepting (P_R) means having to quantify into predicate position – which is unintelligible or in some other way unaccept-able – that view on predication should be rejected. That quantification into predicate position is unintelligible is then a non-question-begging reason to prefer a view on the nature and function of predicates where that nature is *fully* captured by (P_D). It is also the reason Quine gave for why he wouldn't consider using second-order predicate logic when laying bare the logical form of the true statements of our best theory (cf., e.g., Quine 1970). The problem with this view is simply that most seem to think that it is false. Quantification into predicate position is most likely not unintelligible and it is most likely not unacceptable for some other reason either (more on this in Section 3.4.2).

You might think that, since understanding predication in the quinean sense turns explanation implausibly on its head, we ought to go for (P_R). Why is a F? Intuitively, the reason why a is F has something to do with (the nature of) a. What the quinean says (at least so one might think), is however not that. Rather, what the quinean says is that *the reason why a is F is that "F" can be truly predicated of a*. This makes it sound as if predicates are not true of objects in virtue of anything having to do with those objects, but rather that those objects have the natures they do in virtue of those predicates being true of them. To use Armstrongian terminology, what accepting the quinean view of predication seemingly entails is that properties are "nothing but a shadow cast upon particulars by predicates" (1978a: 13). And this is absurd.

That this is absurd can of course be questioned. However, even supposing that it is, the quinean view of predication in all likelihood *does not* entail the (absurd) view that properties are shadows of predicates. What (an instance of)

---

[32] Russell – the "inventor" of the logical analysis of our statements later adopted by Quine – in fact accepted a view of predicate reference along something like these lines. According to Russell, every word has the meaning it does in virtue of "standing for" or "picking out" something in the world (which was why he saw the need to "paraphrase away" definite descriptions). As late as 1912, Russell writes (cf. also Macbride 2006): "Suppose, for instance, that I am in my room. I exist, and my room exists; but does 'in' exist? Yes, obviously the word 'in' has meaning; it denotes a relation which holds between me and my room" (1912: 50).

(P_D) says is that "F" is true of *a* iff *a* is F. It does not say *in virtue of what a* is F. Suppose you're an ostrich nominalist. Then, even so, it does not say that it has to be in virtue of "F" being true of it that *a* is F. According to this kind of nominalist, what exists when "*a* is F" is true is *a*. But then, if anything "makes" *a* be F, it must be *a*. Or, rather, it must be *a* being primitively the way *a* is. Which is not absurd.

I'm *not* saying that there can be no other (conclusive) reason(s) for preferring the quinean view of predication to (P_R) or vice versa. All I'm saying is that, so long as those reasons remain unidentified, how we should view the nature and function of predicates remains an open question. Opting for the quinean view *because properties don't exist* or for the realistic view *because they do* is, moreover, not an option. Whatever reason(s) we cite for preferring one view on the nature and function of predicates over another must be independent of which view on the existence of properties we happen to prefer.

3.4.2 Logics

When the quinean turns simple subject-predicate sentences into existential generalizations – thereby revealing that what those sentences ontologically commit us to does not include properties – he takes for granted that the logic in terms of which those sentences real structure is best expressed is *first-order predicate logic*. What would happen if he chose to express the underlying or real structure of those sentences using *second-order* logic instead? A lot. For, if the logic is second order, what, for example, "*a* is F" ontologically commits us to is no longer that there is *something* that is F. Rather, what that statement says is that (this particular formulation is adapted from Mellor and Oliver [1997: 15]; cf. Jones [2018] for a recent more sophisticated suggestion along these lines; cf. also Macbride [2006: 440] for a discussion):

(4') there is *something* such that "is F" designates it and "*a*" falls under it

And now we can see that our choice of logic matters. For, given that the logical form of (4) is captured using first-order predicate logic, what that statement ontologically commits us to is whatever *a* is, whereas, given that it is captured using second-order logic, what we end up ontologically committed to is the sort of thing "is F" designates.

As noted in the previous section, Quine thought that opting for first-order logic over second-order logic could be independently justified. At one point he claims that this choice is justified by the fact that "it is built into the very distinction between names and predicates that the former but not the latter are susceptible of quantification" (1969: 95). And in a later text, Quine explains why more precisely predicates are not "susceptible of quantification":

> Predicates have attributes as their "intensions" or meanings (or would if there were attributes), and they have sets as their extensions; but they are names of neither. Variables eligible for quantification therefore do not belong in predicate position. They belong in name positions. (1970: 67)

The problem is that these are reasons for rejecting second-order logic only if we have already decided to do so. As noted by Macbride (2006: 442ff.), just because first-order quantifiers range over items that could be named by names, it does not follow that all quantification works that way. And even if you think that naming is somehow necessary for reference, or that whatever our second-order quantifiers range over cannot be named and so cannot be "referred to," this doesn't mean that those things cannot be picked out or ontologically committed to by being bound by second-order quantifiers. Saying that it does begs the question.

I have said far from enough to justify the conclusion that opting for first-order over second-order predicate logic *cannot* be non-question-beggingly justified. The point I want to make is rather that it seems to me as if whether it can or not is, once again, an open question. And since it is an open question the answer to which will decide if properties exist, the question whether properties exist remains open as well.

3.5 Going Linguistic: Summing Up

In this section we have considered what it means to "go linguistic." As I've tried to demonstrate, going linguistic means having your ontological conclusions depend, not just on language, but on how in particular you happen to view the nature and function of language. If I accept a revolutionary approach to paraphrase, first, it does not seem as if going linguistic can tell me *either* that properties exist *or* that they don't. If I conceive of paraphrase hermeneutically, *what* a close study of language can tell me about the existence or not of properties will depend on some other assumptions I make. It will depend on my views on predicate reference. It will depend on my tolerance for second-order logic. It will depend on if I think the problem of symmetry can be overcome, as well as on *how* exactly I overcome it. And so on.

That going linguistic makes whatever ontological conclusions you draw depend heavily on controversial assumptions does not in itself make the approach especially problematic: *every* theory in ontology and metaphysics depends heavily on controversial assumptions, only different ones. What *is* cause for at least some concern is the circumstance that the assumptions in fact made by participants in these debates often seem to lack non-question-begging rationale.

Perhaps this is unavoidable. Then what ontological conclusions we can draw from a close study of language will depend on which ontological beliefs we have going in. But then what justifies *those* beliefs? If no non-question-begging linguistic rationale is available, this justification must be nonlinguistic.

4 Going Nonlinguistic

Here's where we're at: in Section 2 we distinguished between two types of fact giving rise to two types of problem of properties – the linguistic fact of the One over Many and the experiential fact of the One over Many. In Section 3 we critically investigated the prospects of "going linguistic," where to "go linguistic" was understood as accepting the linguistic fact of the One over Many as what gives rise to the problem of properties and then solving (or attempting to solve) *that* problem through a close study of language only.

In this section we investigate the alternative: to "go *non*linguistic."

Given that we have already distinguished the linguistic from the experiential fact of the One over Many, you might think that to "go nonlinguistic" must mean accepting the experiential fact of the One over Many as the fact giving rise to the problem of properties and then accepting that this is a problem that we (attempt to) solve through a close study of *reality*, or of reality as it appears to us *in experience*. You would be wrong. Although going experiential certainly counts as going nonlinguistic, you don't *have to* go experiential to go nonlinguistic.

So what does it take to count as going nonlinguistic? There's no short answer to that question. Some of those I would like to count as going nonlinguistic, first, take the *linguistic* fact of the One over Many as their explanandum (cf. esp. Section 4.2.1). The reason why they nevertheless count as going nonlinguistic is that they do not think that whether properties exist is something you can determine through a close study of language *only*. Some of those I would like to count as going nonlinguistic, second, believe that whether properties exist *is* something we can determine purely linguistically (cf. Section 4.2.2). The reason why they nevertheless count as going nonlinguistic is that they don't think that the interesting or important problem of properties concerns their existence. The interesting and important problem of properties rather concerns their nature, and, they believe, answering questions concerning the nature of properties cannot be done through a close study of language only.

This section has three main parts. The first part (4.1) investigates how issues to do with explanation – what counts as an explanation, what needs to be explained – have made some philosophers go nonlinguistic. The second part (4.2) investigates why those who go nonlinguistic are so deeply skeptical of one assumption going linguistic seemingly requires – that (the structure of) language mirrors (the structure of) reality – as well as what those who reject this Picture Theory of Language propose we put in its stead. The third part (4.3), finally, contains a brief discussion of theory evaluation and theory comparison in a nonlinguistic framework: if we go nonlinguistic, (why) do properties exist?

4.1 Explanation

Those who go nonlinguistic tend to agree with the quinean that the task they are both involved in consists in producing *explanations.* Agreeing on this is, however, perfectly compatible with disagreeing both on *what counts as an explanation* and on *what needs explaining.* I deal with both types of disagreement in what follows.

4.1.1 No Explanation

According to the ostrich nominalist, what analyzing a statement like "*a* and *b* have the same property, F-ness" ultimately reveals is that what must exist for that statement to be true is whatever "*a*" and "*b*" respectively pick out. Does the existence of *a* and *b* *explain why* "*a* and *b* have the same property, F-ness"? According to Armstrong, it doesn't. The Moorean task, he points out, was to explain why *a* and *b* are *the same.* To count as an explanation, therefore, whatever you propose must – obviously! – "consider what sameness of type is" (Armstrong 1980: 442). To answer that *a* and *b* exist is not to consider what sameness of type is. Therefore, to answer that *a* and *b* exist is not to explain why "*a* and *b* have the same property, F-ness."

Is it fair to say that the quinean doesn't even *consider* what sameness of type is? I don't think so. So, for instance, does Quine tell us that: "[t]hat the houses and roses and sunsets are all of them red *may be taken as ultimate*" (1948: 30, emphasis added). I think this proves that he (along with his fellow quineans) *does* consider what sameness of type is. It's just that what considering this leads him to conclude is that it's "ultimate" or "brute" or "primitive."[33]

If the quinean *considers* sameness of type – if only to mutter, "it's ultimate" – does he thereby *explain* what sameness of type is? Armstrong doesn't think so: to him, saying "it's ultimate" or "it's primitive" or "it's brute"

---

[33] More precisely, the quinean claim is that this is brute because what statements of the form "*a* and *b* have the same property, F-ness" really say is that "*a* is F and *b* is F," *which is brute* (thanks to an anonymous reviewer for this Element for pushing me to clarify this).

doesn't count as giving an explanation. According to the quinean, however, it does. Here's why:

> There are three ways to give an account. (1) "I deny it" – this earns a failing mark if the fact is really Moorean. (2) "I analyse it thus" – this is Armstrong's response to the facts of apparent sameness of type. Or (3) "I accept it as primitive". Not every account is an analysis! A system that takes certain Moorean facts as primitive and unanalyzed cannot be accused of failing to make a place for them. It neither shirks the compulsory question nor answers it by denial. It does give an account. (Lewis 1983: 352)

(How) can explanation be brute? Brute facts admittedly lack explanation *in other terms*. There is nothing distinct from a brute fact to which we can point and say: it is *in virtue of that thing (or those things!) that this fact obtains or is true!*[34] Finding out in virtue of what a fact obtains or is true would be enlightening. But so – arguably – would finding out that a fact is fundamental: it would enlighten us about *the nature of (fundamental) reality* (cf. Barnes 1994 for a view along these lines). If to be brute is to be fundamental, and if finding out that something is fundamental is enlightening, then to say of a fact that it is brute *is* to explain that fact. If to explain is to enlighten, that is.

Is to explain to enlighten? Perhaps. What is the nature of explanation, including what is the nature of metaphysical explanation (which is arguably the kind of explanation Moorean facts like that of the One over Many demand) is difficult to say.[35] It does not seem too far-fetched to think that explanation is something that increases our understanding, however. And even if it isn't, even if (metaphysical) explanation is (just) explanation in terms of what grounds what (cf. Section 4.2.2), an explanation identifying some fact as fundamental might count as an explanation even in that sense.[36]

Suppose you're still not sold on the idea of brute explanations. Then note that they may be unavoidable. After all, *every* theory will have to consider *something* as brute or fundamental. Take for example Armstrong's own explanation of the fact of the One over Many. Armstrong (non-brutely) explains this fact in terms of something further: universals. *a* and *b* have what appears to be the same

---

[34] Supposing, that is, that the explanation we seek is not causal but metaphysical.

[35] What *is* a metaphysical explanation? That's a difficult question. Here we can answer it vaguely by saying that a metaphysical explanation is *not* a causal explanation, and that it is most likely an explanation in terms of what (non-causally) "makes" something exist, possibly by constituting that thing (cf., e.g., Brenner et al. 2021 for a recent overview of the ways the nature of metaphysical explanation can be understood).

[36] That is, even if it isn't an explanation in terms of what, besides the fact we want explained, grounds or makes that fact exist, it is still an explanation informing us that *nothing* grounds or "makes" that fact exist. And in this sense at least it is still an explanation in terms of what grounds what.

nature, F-ness, because there is something – the universal F-ness – that exists in *a* and that exists in *b*, *by being instantiated by both*. But what about this fact? (How) does Armstrong explain the fact that universal F-ness is instantiated in both *a* and *b*? Briefly put: "[h]e doesn't" (Lewis 1983: 353).[37] According to Armstrong, the fact that "*a* and *b* instantiate universal F-ness" is brute.

(Why) is this a reason to think that explanation can be brute? According to Lewis, it is a reason to think so because *it would be absurd* if the circumstance that Armstrong takes some facts to be brute counted against his view (254). Does accepting that explanation can be brute mean that the ostrich is off the hook? Not necessarily. That explanation can be brute does not mean that everything is apt to be brutely explained. The fact of the One over Many and the fact that *a* and *b* instantiate universal F-ness are different kinds of facts. The fact of the One over Many is a Moorean fact. The instantiation fact, on the other hand, because it doesn't belong to common sense, because it isn't a fact which truth we cannot doubt or that we take for granted, is most likely *not* a Moorean fact. But then, even if some explanations can be brute, perhaps calling a fact Moorean means that its explanation must be substantial. In which case it would still be true that the quinean "explanation" doesn't count.

Can explanation be brute? Can explanation of Moorean facts be brute? I happen to lean toward a "yes" and a "yes". But I also don't think that very much depends on how we answer those questions here. Why not? Because, if you want to object to the explanations proposed by those who go linguistic, there are more powerful ways to do so.

To see this, we need to consider what it is that turns the fact of the One over Many into *a problem*. As Rodriguez-Pereyra notes in his influential paper "What Is the Problem of Universals?" (2000), how we answer this question will depend on what we mean by "problem." Here's what he thinks we should mean: a fact constitutes a (philosophical) problem if we can ask, of that fact, *how it can obtain (or be true) given certain other things*. What other things? According to Rodriguez-Pereyra (taking his cue from Nozick 1981: 9), the other things are the fact's "apparent excluders." For a fact to turn into a problem, in other words, the coexistence of that fact and that fact's "apparent excluders" must be puzzling. Solving a philosophical problem – explaining a philosophical fact – will then consist in demonstrating one of two things: that the "excluders" only apparently exist, or that they only apparently exclude.

According to the quinean, the fact that turns into a problem is this one:

(4) *a* and *b* have the same property, F-ness.

---

[37] In Armstrong's own words: "[S]uppose we have that *a* instantiates F or that *a* and *b* in that order instantiate R. Do we have to advance any further? I do not think that we do" (1989: 107).

If "problem" is understood as Rodriguez-Pereyra suggests, (4) turns into a problem because it allows us to ask: *how can a and b both be F – how can they be the same – if they are also different?* According to the quinean, if anything explains (4), it must be the existence of *a* and *b*. But, according to Rodriguez-Pereyra, this answer will only do if it can rule out (4)'s "apparent excluders." According to Rodriguez-Pereyra, however, it cannot. Why not? Because of how ontological commitments work. A statement's ontological commitments are those things that must exist for the statement to be true. A statement is in other words ontologically committed to some entity if and only if the truth of that statement *entails* that the entity in question exists. But:

> ... if S entails but is not entailed by "E exists," E's existence does not explain how the fact that S is possible. For then E's existence is compatible with the non-existence of the fact that S and therefore with this fact's *real* excluders, and so E's existence is not enough to explain how the fact that S is possible. (261)

In this particular case if "*a* and *b* are both F" entails that *a* and *b* exist, yet the existence of *a* and *b* does not entail that "*a* and *b* are both F" (which it doesn't because either or both of *a* and *b* could have been differently natured), then the existence of *a* and *b* is compatible with the falsity of "*a* and *b* are both F" and therefore with this fact's *real* excluders. Which means that, if to count as an explanation means *ruling out* that any of a fact's "apparent excluders" is real, listing a statement's ontological commitments *cannot* count as an explanation.[38]

If Rodriguez-Pereyra is right, this is very bad news for those intent on going linguistic. Whether he *is* right will, among other things, depend on if we are willing to accept his views on what counts as a problem as well as on what counts as a solution to a problem. Rodriguez-Pereyra thinks we ought to accept these views because he thinks we ought to think of the project we are involved in when doing ontology as one of producing *truthmakers* for known truths. We'll have to wait until Section 4.2.1 to see if we find that idea compelling or not.

4.1.2 Wrong Explanandum

There are several reasons why you might think that those who go linguistic either explain the wrong thing or that they don't explain everything that needs

---

[38] Here's a possible quinean rejoinder suggested to me by an anonymous reviewer for this Element: to say that the quinean explains (4) by positing the existence of *a* and *b* is to misconstrue his view. After all, the quinean is not saying that *the existence* of houses and sunsets is what is brute or ultimate. Rather, what is brute is *that the house is red* and *that the sunset is red*. But then what explains (4) is not the existence of *a* and *b* but those facts, and those facts are incompatible with (4)'s real excluders. Maybe this solves the problem at hand. However, as we shall see next (Section 4.1.2), it also lands the quinean in new and probably even more serious trouble.

explaining. One such reason was first suggested by Lewis (1983). According to Lewis, although the quinean seems to think it is, the problem of properties is *not* to explain (4). Rather, it is to explain:

(8) *a* and *b* have some common property (are somehow of the same type)

Here's how I understand why Lewis thinks this: even if you take the linguistic fact of the One over Many as your explanandum, you do so because you believe that this fact represents the commonsense fact that many things can all have what appears to be the same nature. Which kind of statement can capture that fact? Not (4). The reason why not is that (4) is hostage to what we happen to have words for. (4) represents the commonsense fact that many things can all have what appears to be the same nature by saying that many things can be described using the same word ("F-ness"). It is, however, doubtful that saying this captures what it was supposed to. (8) on the other hand, because it is "less definite," is not likewise restricted to what we happen to have words for. Which makes it a better pick if what we want to represent is the commonsense fact we began with.

Suppose, therefore, that (8) rather than (4) is the statement we are set to explain. According to Lewis, switching from (4) to (8) is bad news for the quinean, at least it is bad news for the quinean ostrich. Why? Because, if what (8) says is that *a* and *b* are *somehow* the same, the truth of (8) is compatible with a situation where there is no word available to describe how *a* and *b* resemble. But then (8) cannot be paraphrased as:

(5) *a* and *b* are both F

Which means that what (8) says is not just that:

(6) *a* is F, and

(7) *b* is F

But if it isn't, the quinean cannot with justification claim that what (8) onto-logically commits us to is (just) *a* and *b*.[39]

Another reason to think that the Moorean fact in need of explanation is something other or more than what those who go linguistic think it is, is provided by Rodriguez-Pereyra (2000). As we have seen, the quinean identifies the fact of the One over Many with (4), then paraphrases (4) as (5), which,

---

[39] Devitt argues that even if Lewis is right, and (4) ought to be replaced with (8), a paraphrase of that statement exists that allows (a version of) the original argument to go through (Devitt 2010: 28). On this version, (8) is paraphrased as (8') "*a* and *b* significantly resemble each other." If Devitt wants to remain an ostrich nominalist, this most likely will not help, however. For, as noted by Edwards: "this is, in effect, a form of *resemblance nominalism*, which *does* attempt an account of what properties are" (2014: 78).

because it is a hidden conjunction, breaks down into (6) and (7). It is these two simple predications that the quinean then mines for ontological commitments. The result: what explains (6) is the existence of a, what explains (7) is the existence of b, and that a and b are "both F" is taken as ultimate.

Does this generalize? That is, can the quinean take any pair of simple predications, mine them for ontological commitments, and then conclude that whatever those two statements ontologically commit him to explains their conjunction? According to Rodriguez-Pereyra, we have reason to believe he cannot. To see this, consider the following pair of statements (which conjunction Rodriguez-Pereyra refers to as the fact of the Many over One):

(6) a is F, and

(9) a is G

If what (6) ontologically commits us to is the existence of a then, by parity of reasoning, so does (9). And if what two simple predications ontologically commit us to *explains* their conjunction, that a exists must be what explains that "a is F" and that "a is G." But does it really?

One way of putting what seems to be missing here is in terms of how this explanation *differs* from the analogous explanation of (6) and (7). When I explain (6) and (7) with reference to what are those statements' ontological commitments, I explain two distinct truths with reference to two distinct things: a and b. When I explain (6) and (9) the same way, I explain two distinct truths with reference to one and the same thing: a. But how can a (being the way a is) explain the truth of (6) *and* the truth of distinct and different (9)? One way one might think it could is if we were to introduce *ways a is* as part of our explanans. For most quineans, though, this is out of the question.

Another way of putting what's going on here is in terms of Rodriguez-Pereyra's ideas about explanation. According to Rodriguez-Pereyra, as we have seen, to count as such, an explanation must rule out all "apparent excluders." As we have seen, if the problem is that of the One over Many, the "apparent excluder" is the fact that a and b are different. If the problem is that of the Many over One, it is that a and a are the same: how can a and a be different in spite of being the same? Even if we insist that positing (brutely natured) a and b addresses the former problem (cf. fn. 38) the problem of the Many over One remains. From the fact (if it is a fact) that a (being the way a is) explains (6) and the fact that a (being the way a is) explains (9), it does not follow that a (being the way a is) explains the conjunction of (6) and (9).

Can this line of argument be resisted? According to Macbride (2002), it can. Irrespective of whether the puzzle arises from the fact that a and b are different *in spite of being the same* or if it arises from the fact that *a* and *a* are the same *in spite of being different*, the puzzle can be solved purely linguistically. How? By engaging in simple conceptual analysis. For according to Macbride, more precisely, to solve either the problem of the One over Many or the problem of the Many over One, all you need to do is note that sameness and difference can be either numerical or qualitative. As soon as we see this, the "puzzles" disappear. How can *a* and *b* be different in spite of being the same? In virtue of being numerically different yet qualitatively the same. How can *a* and *a* be the same in spite of being different? By being numerically the same yet qualitatively different. Problem (dis)solved (and [dis]solved in a way that doesn't require attention to anything besides language).

Rodriguez-Pereyra disagrees. Sure, numerical difference and sameness are not the same thing as qualitative difference and sameness. However, pointing this out amounts to nothing more than saying that, that *a* and *a* are the same only apparently excludes their being different (or that, that *a* and *b* are different only apparently excludes their being the same). Saying *this* is, however, not the same as saying what numerical and qualitative sameness and difference consists in. We still need to say something about that. And doing so will require more than just conceptual analysis.

At this point I suspect that those who go linguistic might be feeling a bit annoyed, however: "You said that for my explanation to count as an explanation of either the fact of the One over Many or the fact of the Many over One it needed to rule out those facts' 'apparent excluders.' And it does! Because numerical sameness and difference are conceptually distinct from qualitative sameness and difference, those facts' 'apparent excluders' are just that – *apparent*. To now complain that I must *also* say what numerical and qualitative sameness and difference *consist in* is taking things one step too far! I don't owe you an explanation of that. I don't have to play that game."

Let's give those who go linguistic this point.[40] Then consider the following pair of statements (Peacock 2009):

(10) *a* is F and G

---

[40] Indeed, even a property realist might feel the pressure to be generous here. For, as noted by an anonymous reviewer for this Element, if the relevant statements are statements about the nature of properties – say, the nature of tropes – there seems to be a version of the problem of the Many over One facing her as well. To see this, consider the following two truths about one particular trope f_1, truths that, because they concern commonly accepted ideas about the nature of tropes, are acceptable to most trope theorists: (a) trope f_1 is abstract, (b) trope f_1 is particular. (a) and (b) just like (6) and (9) are different truths, yet what explains their truth is the same thing (f_1). Mutatis mutandis for statements about (the nature of) universals (for a discussion of this problem (for tropes), cf. Maurin 2005).

(11) *b* is F but not G

As before, (10) ontologically commits us to *a* and (11) ontologically commits us to *b*. Does the existence of *a* and *b* explain the conjunction of (10) and (11)? That is, does positing *a* and *b* allow us to rule out those statements' "apparent excluders"? No.

Why not? Because, in this case, at least one of the questions we expect our explanation to answer is this: how can *a* and *b* be (qualitatively) the same *in spite of being (qualitatively) different?* Or, if you prefer: how can *a* and *b* be (qualitatively) different *in spite of being (qualitatively) the same?* That neither of these questions can be answered by conceptually distinguishing qualitative sameness and difference from numerical sameness and difference should be obvious.

That it is some combination of facts like (10) and (11) – rather than either the fact of the One over Many or the fact of the Many over One – that needs explaining is a view with some venerable precursors. In, for example, the *Parmenides*, Plato lets Zeno of Elea point out that:

> [I]f things are many, they must then be both like and unlike [Peacock, in his translation, uses "similar" and "dissimilar"], but that is impossible, because unlike things can't be like or like things unlike. (Plato, *Parmenides* 127e: 1–4, cf. Peacock 2009: 215)

If the problem of properties *is* to provide explanations of combinations of facts like (10) and (11) it is unclear how – by purely linguistic means – those who go linguistic can solve it. Which means that this is a reason to go nonlinguistic.

4.1.3 The Nature of Properties

What, more precisely, is it that you have found out if you – on purely linguistic grounds – have found out *that properties exist*? Have you found out what *type* of thing it is that the predicates and/or nominalizations in our language pick out? Only if we have reason to believe that something about the nature of what those terms pick out can be read off the nature of those terms themselves.

As we have seen, property realists differ – sometimes radically – among themselves when it comes to what they take to exist when properties exist. In light of this, it is interesting to note that, among the philosophers who have opted for going linguistic – even among those who have concluded from this that *properties don't exist* – opinions are *not* divided when it comes to the nature of properties. What exists when – or if – properties exist, they agree, are *abstract universals*. How do they know this? If the chosen route is the linguistic one, their answer ought to be: they know this *on the basis of a close study of language.* But this is highly unlikely to be true. In what follows I try to explain why that is.

Take *abstractness* first. On what linguistic grounds can we conclude that properties, if they exist, are abstract? To answer that question, we must first decide what we mean more precisely when we describe properties in this way. Sometimes it sounds as if Quine – and quineans generally – understand by "abstract" *being non-spatiotemporal*. Thus understood, properties exist separated from the spatiotemporal objects that "have" them; they exist "nowhere" and "nowhen," or, as this is sometimes framed, they exist in "Platonic heaven." Thus understood, properties appear to be clearly objectionable creatures. If they exist apart from the objects that have them, they cannot be (directly) perceived, they will lack causal power, and they will be generally really rather difficult to get a grip on. No surprise then that a majority of those who go linguistic think that properties are something to be avoided.

If a close study of our terms *could* reveal that properties are abstract, does this mean that properties are entities that exist apart from the objects that have them, that they are acausal and imperceptible? That depends on what you mean by "abstract." D. C. Williams thought that properties were tropes and that tropes were *abstract* particulars (2018[1953]: 32–33). But Williams didn't think that properties (tropes) existed apart from the objects that have them. The term "abstract," he pointed out, has been used to pick out many and very different things, including being "the product of a magical feat of mind," being "the denzien of some remote immaterial eternity," being "imprecise," being "mental," being "rational," being "incorporeal," being "ideally perfect," being "nontemporal," being "primordial or ultimate," being "deficient," being "potential," being "unreal," being "symbolic, figurative or merely representative," or being "vague, confused and indefinite." When Williams characterized his tropes as abstract, he didn't mean *any* of those things. To him, tropes are rather abstract in the sense in which Campbell – another trope theorist – describes them: by being such that they can only be "brought before the mind … by a process of selection, of systematic setting aside, of … other qualities of which we are aware" (Campbell 1990: 2).[41] But then, *even if* that properties are abstract was something that could be decided linguistically, unless that pronouncement was further specified, it wouldn't really tell us anything in particular about the nature of properties.

---

[41] To add to the confusion: that tropes are abstract in no more than the sense specified by Williams and Campbell has led some trope theorists to prefer categorizing tropes as concrete (cf., e.g., Küng 1967 and Giberman 2014).

Can whether properties are abstract be gleaned from a close study of language? At least some of the things van Inwagen – a devoted quinean *and* a property realist – has said indicate that it can. According to van Inwagen, there are statements that seemingly refer to properties, where this seeming reference cannot be paraphrased away. So properties exist. According to van Inwagen, moreover, when properties exist something abstract exists (and – thinks van Inwagen – when something abstract exists, something that exists apart from the object that "has it," something non-spatiotemporal, acausal, and imperceptible, exists). Why think that properties are abstract? Van Inwagen admits that a purely quinean analysis is not enough to inform us about the nature of properties. Given some of the other things he says, however, he seems committed to the view that a close study of language – only not (just) a quinean analysis of it – *can* justify thus characterizing properties. He explains that:

> [I]t is possible to divide the terms and predicates we use in everyday and scientific and philosophical discourse into two exhaustive and exclusive classes by a very simple method. We stipulate that one class shall contain the terms and predicates in the following list: "table," "the copy of *War and Peace* on the table," "Mont Blanc," "the Eiffel Tower," "Catherine the Great," "neutron star," "intelligent Martian," "elf," "angel," "god," and "God." We stipulate that the other shall contain "number," "the ratio of 1 to 0," "proposition," "sentence" ... "property," "angle" ... "possibility" ... [etc.] We then ask philosophers ... to place each term of our discourse ... in the class where it will be most at home. (2004: 108–109)

To be something picked out by a term belonging to the first box is what it is to be concrete. And to be something picked out by a term belonging to the second box is what it is to be abstract. Properties are abstract, van Inwagen tells us, because "property" belongs in the second box. And properties *exist*, if "at least some of the linguistic items in the second box really are terms (really are predicates) and really have referents (really have non-empty extensions)" (109).

What happens if we don't agree about what goes in which box? Van Inwagen willingly admits that disagreement happens. One example he gives is this:

> Most philosophers would put "{Catherine the Great, {the Eiffel Tower}}" in with "property" and "the lion"; but the author of *Parts of Classes* might be inclined to think that this term was more at home with "Catherine the Great" and "the Eiffel Tower." (109)[42]

---

[42] The author of *Parts of Classes* (1991) is David Lewis and, in that book, he argues for the – admittedly idiosyncratic – view that set theory is entangled with mereology.

Does "{Catherine the Great, {the Eiffel Tower}}" belong in the abstract or in the concrete box? On van Inwagen's view, this will depend on what that term picks out. More precisely, it will depend on if what that term picks out is understood along the lines of *Parts of Classes* or if it is understood instead in a more conventional way. But if this is how we find out whether sets are abstract or concrete, there is trouble. For now we can imagine that you and I disagree about where to put "is olive green." If where to put "is olive green" depends on how we understand the nature of the thing "is olive green" picks out, ours is *not* a disagreement about the nature of words. If anything, it is a disagreement about the nature of the sort of thing certain words pick out. Which means that *whether* what "is olive green" picks out is abstract or concrete depends on what the nature of that thing happens to be. But then, rather than a way to draw conclusions about the nature of properties from the nature of our terms, the putting into boxes of words *presupposes* knowledge of that nature (Maurin 2020).

Now consider *universality*. Suppose predicates refer to, or otherwise ontologically commit us to, properties. Unlike, for example, singular terms, predicates are general terms. Generality is "like" universality: general terms can be "true of" more than one singular term just like a universal can be exemplified by more than one object. Given their similarity, can we conclude from the nature of predicates that, if predicates refer, what they refer to is universal? I don't think so. At least not if what we mean when we say of something that it is "universal" is restricted to it being *something able to exist fully in more than one place at one moment in time*. For, *even if* whatever our predicates refer to (if they refer) must be something that makes sense of the fact that the same predicate can be true of more than one singular term, what our predicates refer to may be one of the many types of entity we find in the literature "simulating" the universality of universals. This includes, for example, resemblance classes of objects, or resemblance classes of tropes, or even classes of objects formed on *on the basis of* which predicate is true of them (which would make properties shadows of predicates).[43]

In any case, very few quineans who think properties exist think so because they believe that predicates refer to properties. Rather, they think properties exist because they fail to paraphrase away seeming reference to properties by terms in the subject position. Are those terms general terms? Judging from

---

[43] To reinforce this point: given that we're taking the mark of universality to be the capacity to exist fully at more than one place at a time (and given that we understand "exist fully" to preclude ordinary material objects from satisfying the characterization), it seems we must count entities that prima facie do not seem to have anything to do with tracking co-predication as universal (example: multi-locator extended simple material objects). Thanks to an anonymous reviewer for this Element for pointing this out.

where they appear in the statement, it would seem that they are not. Perhaps the fact that they are the product of a process of nominalization to which a predicate has been subjected means that they in some sense are. In any case, this is at least unclear. And *if* those terms are not general terms, that language commits us to properties gives us *no* special reason to think that what language thereby commits us to is something universal.

If we want the nature of predicates to be able to inform us about the nature of properties, finally (and, assuming that properties are somehow different from objects), the linguistic distinction between singular terms and predicates had better be a clean one. However, as famously argued by Ramsey (1925, cf. also Macbride 2005a and 2005b), it does not seem as if it is. Ramsey asks us to compare two seemingly distinct and different subject-predicate statements:

(12) Socrates is wise

(13) wisdom is a characteristic of Socrates

If the distinction between subject and predicate is what Ramsey calls "logical," (12) and (13) should say different things. But Ramsey doesn't think that they do. Rather, he thinks that:

> [T]he two sentences . . . assert the same fact and express the same proposition. They are not, of course, the same sentence, but they have the same meaning, just as two sentences in two different languages can have the same meaning. (404)

To Ramsey this means that the distinction between subject and predicate is a mere surface or grammatical distinction that does not reflect any real difference between subject and predicate. Ramsey concludes:

> [T]here is no essential distinction between the subject of a proposition and its predicate, and no fundamental classification of objects can be based upon such a distinction. (404)

If Ramsey is right, the whole project of finding out about what distinguishes properties from the objects that "have" them by looking at what distinguishes predicates from singular terms is a nonstarter.

In this section I have argued that going linguistic doesn't allow you to say anything whatsoever about the nature of properties. Those who go linguistic claim either that *properties exist* or that *they don't*. How can they make these claims if they cannot say what it is they thereby either accept or reject the existence of? The short answer is that they *cannot* claim this if they cannot say what it is they either accept or reject the existence of: they must be able to say at least *something* about the nature of properties. Which requires "going nonlinguistic."

4.2 Framework Assumptions

Most of those who go nonlinguistic do not do this because they first tried very hard to go linguistic, failed, and then grudgingly opted for the alternative. Most who go nonlinguistic rather do so because they are deeply skeptical of the idea that what there is, is anything that can be decided through a close study of language. *That* what there is can be decided through a close study of language, they point out, depends on our accepting what is sometimes called the Picture Theory of Language. But this theory is implausible, perhaps even manifestly incorrect.

What does the Picture Theory of Language *say*? Since there is more than one way this theory can be understood, this is not a question with one determinate answer. A good place to start is with Wittgenstein's (1922) version of the view (although, for the record, Heil [2003] thinks that metaphysics has been under the influence of something like the Picture Theory at least since Kant). In Wittgenstein's version, the Picture Theory of Language says that the meaning of a sentence is just what it "pictures" and that what it "pictures" is *how the world is structured, if the sentence is true* (cf. Jago 2006 for a good first introduction to the Wittgensteinian view). What the Picture Theory prescribes is, in other words, that *the structure* of language mirrors *the structure* of reality. In this, the way language pictures reality is more like how a diagram pictures reality and less like how a naturalist painting does. It is *because* language mirrors reality in this structural sense that studying the structure of the former can tell us about the structure of the latter (at least, this is why it can tell us how reality *would be* structured had the sentences studied been true).

Do those who go linguistic accept something like this view on the relationship between language and reality? Yes. Although, as we have seen, hardly anyone "going linguistic" thinks we can read off the structural features of reality from the structural features of language *directly*, accepting something like the quinean view means accepting that, to find out about reality, we must first unveil (and then study) the underlying logical structure of our statements: this structure and not the structure we find, so to speak, "on the surface" mirrors the corresponding (categorical) structure of reality. Which is also why these philosophers think studying the former can inform us about the latter.

Heil – an ardent critic of the view – thinks the Picture Theory ought to be rejected quite simply because it is "manifestly incorrect" (2003: 5). One reason he gives for this claim – a reason of immediate relevance for the topic of this Element, moreover – is that "[a] corollary of the Picture Theory" is that "to every meaningful predicate there corresponds a property" (6). Which is "manifestly incorrect."

Heil's is *not* a good reason for rejecting the Picture Theory, however. First, because, even if it is manifestly incorrect that to every meaningful predicate there corresponds a property, this is most likely not something to which the Picture Theory of Language commits us. To see why, consider the quinean. Although he accepts that the structure of logically regimented language mirrors the structure of reality – although he accepts something along the lines of the (Wittgensteinian) Picture Theory of Language – he doesn't accept that to every meaningful predicate there corresponds a property. Why not? Basically, because he doesn't think of predicates as referring devices in the first place. And although he *does* accept that in cases where a statement's subject-term features a nominalization, that nominalization might correspond to or pick out a property, he doesn't even accept that to every meaningful *nominalization* there corresponds a property. This is because the quinean accepts paraphrase. That is, he accepts that *before* we can study the structure of language in order to find out about the structure of reality, we must make sure we have exhausted all our paraphrasing options. *That* a nominalization features in a true meaningful statement hence does not guarantee that it picks out a property.

But then either quineanism does not presuppose the Picture Theory of Language or it presupposes a different version of that theory than the one targeted by Heil's criticism. We have reason to believe that quineanism *does* presuppose a – Wittgensteinian – version of the Picture Theory. Therefore, the version of that theory Heil has in mind is most likely *not* Wittgensteinian. Then what is it?

According to Heil, the Picture Theory is a "family of loosely related doctrines," the core idea of which is that "the character of reality can be 'read off' our linguistic representations of reality" (2003: 6). In light of the sorts of reasons he then presents against that theory, this should probably be read as saying that the Picture Theory is a view on which *both* the structure and the content of reality is mirrored by language. This makes his version of the Picture Theory considerably more demanding than the Wittgensteinian one.

Does anyone presuppose Heil's version of the Picture Theory? If taken in full generality, probably not. It is after all well known that a view on which every meaningful predicate picks out a property ends up in contradiction or paradox.[44] The way I read Heil's opposition to the Picture

---

[44] Cf. Bolander 2017. If you're a beginner to the paradoxes of self-reference, you might want to start with McDaniel (2020: 44–46).

Theory, its main target are views that at least moderately reasonable people have found it worthwhile to defend. Therefore, Heil most likely doesn't intend the view he criticizes to be taken in full generality: even if that view is accepted, therefore contradiction and paradox-inducing predicates like "is round and square" or "is non-self-exemplifying" *do not* correspond to a property.

Here are a couple of predicates that *do*, however (this list comes from Lewis [1983: 345]):

> not golden
> golden or wooden
> metallic
> self-identical
> owned by Fred
> belonging to class C (where C is an "utterly miscellaneous class")
> grue[45]
> first examined before 2000 A.D.
> being identical
> being alike in some respect
> being exactly alike
> being part of
> owning
> being paired with by some part in R (where R is an "utterly miscellaneous class")

Is the view that these predicates (and more!) correspond to properties "manifestly incorrect"? That depends on what you mean by "property." According to Lewis, "property" is a word for classes – any classes – of things, and "to have a property" is to be a member of a class. Properties, thus understood, are what Lewis calls "abundant":[46]

> Any class of things, be it ever so gerrymandered and miscellaneous and indescribable in thought and language, and be it ever so superfluous in characterising the world, is nevertheless a property. (346)

Properties, in this sense of the word, are not to be conflated with universals. Universals, says Lewis, are "sparse." They are what ground the causal powers of and objective resemblances between things. They are what carves reality at its joints. If saying that every meaningful predicate corresponds to a property means saying that every meaningful predicate corresponds to *a universal* (or whatever else you take to fill the role of the world's sparse properties), what you are saying does

---

[45] "Grue" is a made-up predicate introduced in Goodman 1955. An object is grue if and only if it is either green and has been observed before now, or blue and has not been observed before now.

[46] For an introduction to the distinction between sparse and abundant properties, cf. Orilia and Paolini Paoletti 2020: section 3.2. Cf. also Schaffer 2004.

seem to be "manifestly incorrect." For, clearly, "being golden or wooden" or "being grue" is not being in a way that carves reality at its joints. But if what you mean is rather that to every meaningful predicate corresponds a property in the sense of *a class of* – possibly gerrymandered and miscellaneous – entities, what you say, although it may be incorrect, is at least not "*manifestly* incorrect." Add to this the fact that most (perhaps all) of those who *do* accept that all (noncontradictory or non-paradox-inducing) predicates correspond to a property mean by this "property" in precisely this watered-down, non-natural, or second-class sense. Then Heil's criticism of the Picture Theory does not even threaten those who think that to every predicate corresponds a property. Therefore Heil's is not a good reason to reject either version of the Picture Theory of Language.

Granted this, and granted that the Picture Theory presupposed by the quinean is Wittgensteinian, what *would* constitute a reason to be skeptical of that theory? According to the Picture Theory, the structure of language mirrors the structure of reality. On this view, therefore, it just so happens that language (a human artifact) has evolved in a way that has made it structurally isomorphic to the reality it represents (or so one might think). One reason to be skeptical of the Picture Theory, thus understood, is then that, because language serves many functions, of which representing reality is but a – possibly minor – one, it seems unlikely that language would have evolved in this way. Clearly we need to be able to represent reality in order to "get around," but why should this entail that the way we represent that reality *mirrors* what it is fundamentally (structurally) like?[47]

Why "or so one might think"? Because, as it turns out, although it makes sense to think that *if* the Picture Theory of Language is true, language must have evolved in the way just described, if you're a quinean, it couldn't have. According to the quinean, the structure of language, at least the structure of language *as it appears to us on its surface* (which happens to be language *as we*

---

[47] What if language is not a human artifact but rather an abstract object that we humans use? An anonymous reviewer for this Element asks whether such a view on the nature of language might not lend some credence to the thought that "significant underlying logical structures across all the languages (or all the languages of some significant type) do in some sense mirror fundamental reality." The idea would then be that we gravitate toward some languages *because* they have an underlying reality-mirroring structure. I admit that it is possible that language is not a human artifact. I doubt, though, that if it is not, this would lend the Picture Theory any special credence. Primarily this is because it does not seem to me (and for the same reasons it didn't when I consider language a human artifact) as if how we use language (even if we're not its creators) gives us any reason to prefer a language that has an underlying reality-mirroring structure over one that doesn't. And I cannot come up with any other nonarbitrary reason to think that language would have such a structure – that is, one that doesn't refer to our use of language (although that I cannot is no proof that no such reason exists, of course!). In any case, if (*pace* what I just said) it turns out that accepting a view of language as an abstract entity is the only way the mirror thesis could be justified, this means that to go linguistic *presupposes* the existence of something abstract. I guess some nominalists might have a problem with that.

use it in our everyday lives) doesn't mirror the structure of reality. Which is why the quinean thinks that we – to find out what kinds of things our true statements ontologically commit us to – must *disregard* those statements' (surface) structure. But if language did not evolve this way, *why* think that its – underlying – logical structure mirrors the structure of the reality it represents? This is now a complete mystery. And, even if you're skeptical of the idea that language evolved in a way that made its structure mirror that of reality, saying that it did sure beats having *no* account to give of why the structure of language mirrors the structure of reality. This is therefore *another* reason to be skeptical of the Picture Theory of Language.

I think the sorts of doubts expressed in the previous two paragraphs do have some force. But before we reject the Picture Theory outright, we should acknowledge that doing so leaves a void, a void that *must be* filled. Even Heil admits that his conviction that the Picture Theory should go "does not stem from [his] being in possession of a better, more plausible account of the connection words (or concepts, or thoughts, or representations generally) bear to the world" (2003: 6). Yet, given that the way we speak of reality, along with the way we experience reality and, perhaps, the way we somehow rationally conceive of reality, is the only evidence we have *of what reality is like*, some such account is necessary! Even those hell-bent on getting rid of the Picture Theory nevertheless want their theories to be either scientifically adequate or, at least, they want them to respect a select group of – Moorean – commonsense truths. Even if they are prepared to have both the structure and content of reality differ from the structure and content of the way we represent that reality, therefore, they still expect truth and reality to somehow "line up." But how? It is easy to be critical of the Picture Theory but difficult to find a good replacement for it. In Sections 4.2.1 and 4.2.2 we take a much too brief look at two attempts at such replacement. Before those have been properly tested and evaluated, the fact that going linguistic presupposes accepting something along the lines of the Picture Theory of Language is at most a weak reason against that approach.

4.2.1 Properties As Truthmakers

Rodriguez-Pereyra thinks that a statement's ontological commitments cannot explain why that statement is true (cf. Section 4.1). Why not? Because explanation doesn't work that way: for x to explain the truth of "x exists," x (existing) must entail the truth of that statement, *not the other way around*. What entails the truth of statements? According to the truthmaker theorist, truthmakers do.

Which means that, according to the truthmaker theorist, what explains the truth of a statement like "*a* and *b* have the same property, F-ness," is what makes that statement true.

What does it mean to say of something that it *makes true* a statement? It means that that statement is true *in virtue of* that thing. But what this "in virtue of" picks out is something truthmaker theorists disagree on (cf. Macbride 2021). Some take the relation "in virtue of" picks out as primitive. But even if we agree that it is, this does not absolve us from explaining how it works. In particular, it does not absolve us from explaining why the fact that something makes true "*a* and *b* have the same property, F-ness," means that that thing also *explains* the truth of that statement. Nor, for that matter, does it absolve us from explaining how the circumstance that it makes true (and hence explains) this statement allows us to conclude either that properties exist or that they don't (if it allows us to conclude this, that is).

Early on, philosophers tried to make more precise the idea that truths are true "in virtue of" truthmakers in terms of *entailment*: to say of something that it *makes true* a statement is to say that the existence of that thing *entails* that truth. This way of speaking is now mostly abandoned, however. The reason why is that, according to what is clearly the most common view of "entailment," that term denotes a relation that can only hold between statements or propositions and not, as here, between something in the world and whatever we take to be able to carry a truth-value (Armstrong 2004: 5–6).

Today a majority of the truthmaker theorists therefore prefer describing the truthmaking relation as a *necessitating* relation: to say of something that it *makes true* a statement is to say that the existence of that thing (metaphysically) *necessitates* that truth.[48] Necessitation is a modal relation. It can hold either between items in the world or, as in this case, between items in the world and truthbearers. Necessitation and entailment are closely related: if x – for example, the truthmaker for "that woman's coat is olive green" – exists, the truth of "x exists" *entails* the truth of "that woman's coat is olive green."

In Rodriguez-Pereyra's argument for regarding a statement's truthmakers as what explains that statement's truth, both entailment and necessitation play important roles:

> [O]ne way of explaining how some fact S is possible is by invoking the existence of something which *entails* it. If "E exists" entails S then E's existence *necessitates* the fact that S. ... E's existence rules out the real excluders of the fact that S: what necessitates the fact that S thereby

---

[48] For some exceptions to this rule, cf., for example, Parsons 1999 and Briggs 2012.

"impossibilitates" its real excluders and so explains how S is possible. (2000: 261, emphasis added)

Is saying of the truthmaking relation that it is a necessitating relation enough to ensure that it is also an explanatory relation? Most likely not. Reason: necessary truths. Here's one example:

(14) 2+2=4

This sentence is true no matter what: anything – including, for example, that woman's coat – makes (14) true. But surely that woman's coat doesn't *explain why* "2+2=4" is true! *Even if* the existence of that woman's coat rules out (14)'s real excluders, therefore, since it does so only vacuously ([14] doesn't have any real excluders because [14] is a necessary truth), that the coat exists doesn't explain why (14) is true.

Suppose truthmaking is an explanatory relation. Then something must make the difference between the case where the existence of that woman's coat necessitates the truth of (14) and the case where it necessitates – and thereby *makes true* – "that woman's coat is olive green"?[49] What? Answering this question is surprisingly difficult. One possibility is that what makes the difference is relevance: to count as a truthmaker for a truth, that truthmaker must "in some sense" be what that truth is about (cf. Macbride 2021). This seems to be on the right track, but since words like "relevance" and "about" have unclear meanings it's also unclear if this tells us very much more than that truthmaking is necessitation *plus something else* (which we kind of knew going in!). Another possibility – to be further explored in the next section (4.2.2) – is that we view truthmaking as a kind of grounding. Grounding relations are generally understood as necessitating but not *just* necessitating (or modal) relations (they are what some call "hyperintensional" rather than just "intensional" relations[50]). Does saying that truthmaking is a kind of grounding inform us about what more precisely makes the difference between cases of (explanatory) truthmaking and the case involving (14)? I'm not sure that it does. For what I want to do in what follows, that it might not is probably okay, though. Let's suppose, therefore, that although we cannot say exactly how pure necessitation differs from truthmaking, if truthmaking is to play the explanatory role that, for example, Rodriguez-Pereyra expects it to play, we must say *that* they differ, which means that truthmaking is not just necessitation (it is necessitation⁺).

---

[49] That *just* that woman's coat (and not, e.g., the state of affairs *that that woman's coat exists*) necessitates the truth of "that woman's coat is olive green" is doubtful, though. I'll say more about why in just a moment.

[50] For more on the hyperintensionality of grounding, cf. Bliss and Trogdon 2021, esp. section 2.2. For a more formal introduction to the notion, cf. Berto and Nolan 2021.

The truthmaker view, thus understood, has several prima facie attractive features. As we have seen, Rodriguez-Pereyra argues persuasively for the view that explanation requires necessitation in the direction from what exists to what is true, not the other way around. Truthmaking can give you this. The truthmaker view also allows for what Schaffer has called a "radically minimal ontology without tears" (2008: 9). This is because, although what must exist is what necessitates (or necessitates$^+$) what is true, what it is that thereby exists is not anything that can be "read off" from those truths.

To see this, suppose it's true that "that woman's coat is olive green." What truthmaker theory says is that what makes that statement true necessitates$^+$ that truth. What it doesn't say is that what exists and makes that statement true is anything we can find out by simply checking to see what that statement ontologically commits us to. Among other things, this means that, given truthmaker theory, "that woman's coat is olive green" may be true, yet there are no coats and there are no colors. If there are no coats or colors, what makes that statement true? Perhaps that statement is made true by complexly arranged fundamental particles. Perhaps it is made true by something else. Truthmaker theory can be combined with a radical rejection of the Picture Theory of Language. If it is, the structure and content of what makes a statement true may differ, perhaps radically, from the structure and content of that statement.

One reason to think that properties exist given this way of approaching the task of doing ontology has to do with the fact that the truth of statements like "that woman's coat is olive green" is *contingent*: the statements are true but they could have been false. If I'm a nominalist, I think that "that woman's coat is olive green" is made true by an object – that woman's coat or whatever particles arranged coat-wise exist when that woman's coat seems to exist. Can the existence of that coat (or of those particles) make true "that woman's coat is olive green"? It doesn't seem that it can. Why not? Because the existence of that coat (or of those particles) is compatible with the falsity of "that woman's coat is olive green." In other words, because the coat (or the particles) could have been differently colored, its existence does not *necessitate* the truth of that statement.

What would make true "that woman's coat is olive green"? According to many truthmaker theorists, what must exist for "that woman's coat is olive green" to be true is the coat (or the particles) *being olive green* (or being whichever way science tells us an object is when we describe it as olive green). But this means that, for that statement to be true, not only does there have to be an object, there also has to be a property, and the object must exemplify the property. What makes true simple predications like "that woman's coat is olive green" is therefore what is often referred to as *states of affairs* (cf., e.g., Armstrong 1997).

What exists when a state of affairs exists? The most common view on the nature of states of affairs is the one mentioned in the previous paragraph. On this view, what exists when a state of affairs does is an object or "property bearer" (what Armstrong [1997] calls a "thin particular") and a property (which can be either a universal or a trope) in a "non-mereological mode of composition." But states of affairs can also be understood as tropes, at least if tropes are non-transferable. On this view, what exists when "that woman's coat is olive green" is true is the particular property (the trope) that coat has. On this view, more precisely, since tropes essentially belong together in object-like bundles, all that is required for the truth of that statement is the existence of *that trope* (for more on this version of the trope view, cf. esp. the classic paper by Mulligan, Simons, and Smith 1984).

Does this mean that if you're a truthmaker theorist you must also be a property realist? No. As noted by, for example, Peacock (2009; cf. also Schaffer 2008), claiming that the truthmaker for "that woman's coat is olive green" must be a state of affairs only amounts to claiming *that the truthmaker for that statement must be a state of affairs*. But saying this does not – indeed, it cannot – tell us what a state of affairs *is* (other than negatively: it is not [just] an object). As we have already seen, states of affairs can be construed as complexes involving a property or they can be construed as (nontransferable) tropes. But they don't have to be construed that way. We could regard states of affairs as brutely natured, simple, and sui generis (perhaps along the lines of the "facts" posited in Wittgenstein 1922). We could even think of what plays the role of the state of affairs as a (resemblance)class of objects (which is how Rodriguez-Pereyra [2008: 9] understands the truthmakers in question).

Given truthmaker theory, do properties exist or not? As pointed out by Imaguire (2018: 35), truthmaker theory cannot say. Imaguire sees this as a reason in favor of going linguistic after all. Ontological commitments, he points out, are "univocal": given any set of statements we take to be true, quinean analysis will yield a unique and definitive answer about what there is.

Although Imaguire is right to point out that truthmakers are not univocal – that more than one (kind of) thing can make true our statements – he is, however, wrong if he thinks that this must be a point in the quinean's favor. For, first, it is unclear if the quinean analysis *does* yield a unique and definite answer. At least this is unclear if we take into consideration the fact that what results from such an analysis will depend on which more or less contentious semantic assumptions the quinean makes. In any case, it does not seem as if we can criticize truthmakers for not being univocal. The truthmaker theorist – or, in general, those who go nonlinguistic – tend not to think of what they are doing in terms of coming up with "univocal" answers in the first place. Rather, they think of what they are doing as theorizing about what *can* play various roles, such as the role of truthmakers. If more than one (kind of) thing can play that role, so be it. It's not that the truthmaker theorist is uninterested in questions to do with *which* (kind of) truthmaker we should prefer to posit in our ontology. It's just that this question is not a truthmaker theoretical question. I'll have more to say about what kind of question it is, and how we can go about answering it if the framework is nonlinguistic in Section 4.3. Until then, I suggest we move on.

4.2.2 Properties As Grounds

According to some so-called grounding theorists, reality is hierarchically struc-tured into levels.[51] At the bottom of the hierarchy are the fundamentals.[52] These are entities which existence grounds the existence of other things, but that are not themselves grounded in anything further. The relations that hold between the fundamentals and what they ground, and between that which the fundamen-tals ground and what *they* ground, and so forth, are the *grounding relations*. According to the kind of grounding theorist I have in mind in what follows, grounding is a mind-independent relation that holds between mind-(in)dependently[53] existing entities.[54] The nature of grounding, most of these theor-ists agree, is primitive (brute). There are things we can say about it, though. According to the orthodoxy, grounding always runs in one direction – from the more to the less fundamental – which means that grounding is asymmetric and irreflexive (and transitive, but we don't have to care too much about that here). If x fully grounds y, moreover, x necessitates the existence (and nature) of y. But grounding is not *just* modal (or intensional); it's *hyper*intensional: just because

---

[51] I say "some" because I don't intend what I say here to cover all the ways people have defended grounding. The sort of grounding theorist I have in mind in what follows is a realist, not necessarily about properties, but about grounding and about what grounding relates. Grounding theorists of this type include Schaffer (cf. esp. his 2009), Audi 2012, and Trogdon 2013.

[52] Although the grounding theorist I have in mind here believes that there is a fundamental level, it is probably possible to be a grounding theorist and not believe this. For a good critical investigation of the idea that there must be a fundamental level, cf., for example, Bliss 2019.

[53] That grounding is mind-independent hence does not prevent it from possibly obtaining between states – like, for example, mental or semantic states – that we in one way or another count as mind-dependent (nor, for that matter, does it prevent it from possibly obtaining between those types of states and states that are mind-independent).

[54] A majority of the grounding theorists take the relata of the grounding relation to be *states of affairs*, but, for example, Schaffer (2009) thinks more or less any kind of entity can stand in this type of relation. The grounding theorist I have in mind in what follows can accept either of those views.

x necessitates the existence of y, it doesn't follow that x grounds the existence of y. And just like we discussed in the case of truthmaking, the something extra grounding brings to the table has to do with relevance and explanation. Sometimes this is captured by saying that grounding is non-monotonic (relevance) and explanatory. Because grounding is an explanatory relation, moreover, locutions used to describe it – besides the obvious "grounds" or "is grounded in" – include "exists in virtue of" or "because of" (for a good overview, cf. Bliss and Trogdon 2021).

If you view truthmaking as an intensional relation, you can think of grounding as its more substantial (hyperintensional) cousin. As we have just seen, however, if your intention is to (attempt to) solve the problem of properties by positing truthmakers you'll probably need to think of truthmaking as hyperintensional as well. Which is precisely why some have thought of truthmaking as a special kind of grounding relation.

If truthmaking is a special kind of grounding relation, the way it's special is this: "ordinary" grounding normally relates things that exist in mind-independent reality to less fundamental things that exist in mind-independent reality. If x (fully) grounds y, x makes y *exist and be the way it is.* What we may call "truthmaker-grounding," on the other hand, relates things that exist in mind-independent reality to things like statements or sentences or propositions (in general: representational entities able to carry a truth-value). If x (fully) truthmaker-grounds y, x makes y true (where y is some truthbearer the existence of which is independent of whether it is made true by x).

That truthmaking is a special kind of grounding relation is contentious. Fine (2012: 43–46) – a grounding theorist – finds several faults with that idea, as do some truthmaker theorists (e.g., Heil 2003 and Cameron 2008), then mostly because they don't accept the hierarchical – leveled – conception of reality's structure the grounding framework presupposes (for yet further reasons not to regard truthmaking as a kind of grounding, cf. Audi 2020).

If the setting is grounding theoretical, do properties exist? According to Schaffer (2009), they do. Indeed, that they do is trivial and can be found out using something-from-nothing-transformations of the kind promoted by the (neo)Carnapian (whose views were quickly introduced only to be immediately shelved in the introduction to Section 3). Here's Schaffer's "proof of the existence of properties" (358) (for another example of this sort of transformation, cf. Section 3.3.2):

There are properties that you and I share.
Therefore, there are properties.

If Schaffer thinks we can find out if properties exist by performing simple "derivations" like the one just presented, why doesn't he count as going linguistic? Because to count as going linguistic you must think that solving the problem of properties can be done through a close study of language *only*. Schaffer doesn't think that. He believes that, to find out everything we want to find out about properties (or whatever else we contemplate including in our ontology), we must *first* investigate what language *says* there is. After all, "[t]heories themselves are sentences," which means that "what they commit us to *has to be* at least in part a function of what these sentences mean" (2008: 9). Proceeding linguistically allows us to conclude *that properties exist*. But whether properties exist was never the interesting metaphysical question to begin with! This is because Schaffer thinks that metaphysics deals in substantive questions about which reasonable people may disagree. That properties exist can be easily demonstrated using the "argument" set out previously. Therefore, whether properties exist is *not* anything about which reasonable people may disagree. But then, if there is a *problem* of properties, it cannot concern *that*.

So what does it concern? According to Schaffer – and this is where grounding comes in – the interesting and important question giving rise to the *problem* of properties is this: are properties fundamental? And perhaps also this: if properties are not fundamental, what grounds their existence? When a nominalist says that *properties don't exist*, there are two ways we can interpret him: we can take him to say that properties don't exist on any level of reality (which, according to Schaffer, would make what he says trivially false), or we could take him – as we most likely should – to be saying that properties, although they exist somewhere in the hierarchy, do not exist *on the fundamental level*. Likewise, when a realist says that *properties exist*, although this is compatible with properties existing somewhere in the hierarchy, the most reasonable interpretation of what the realist says is *that properties – which exist – are fundamental*.

Why can't we decide if properties are fundamental or if they exist in virtue of some other kind of entity (and if so which) purely linguistically? According to Schaffer, this is because drawing ontological conclusions from language will at most allow us to produce an – unstructured or "flat" – list of existents. The quinean "task" is, in other words, to:

> ... solve for E = the set (or class or plurality) of entities. There is no structure to E. For any alleged entity, the flat conception offers two classificatory options: either the entity is in E, or not. (354)

Are properties fundamental? Grounding theory arguably cannot say. At least it cannot say *determinately* or *univocally* that properties are fundamental. Or that they aren't. At most, the grounding theorist can hypothesize that reality's structure either does or doesn't include properties on the fundamental level (for a reason to think that it doesn't, cf. Schulte 2019). This is because to "go grounding theoretical" only allows you to "deploy diagnostics for what is fundamental, together with diagnostics for grounding" (351). It does not in itself dictate which diagnostics to accept, and which to discard.[55]

Suppose I diagnose what is fundamental such that properties come out as fundamental. Suppose you don't. Then who is right is not anything we can settle with the help of *more* grounding theoretic diagnostics. Theory comparison and theory choice will be a matter decided – or at least debated – with reference to those theories' theoretical virtues. What this means, as well as what regarding theory comparison and theory choice in this way can tell us about the existence and/or fundamentality of properties is briefly discussed in the next – and final – section.

4.3 Theory Comparison and Theory Choice

Here's what you must do to solve the problem of properties the nonlinguistic way: First, you identify the relevant (Moorean) fact(s) that need explaining (which, as seen in Sections 2.2 and 4.1.2, may require some thought). Once those facts have been identified, you determine which views on the nature and (fundamental) existence of properties would qualify as explanations of those facts. And to be able to do that, you must first decide what *counts* as an explanation (which, as we have seen in Section 4.1, means that you must decide what (metaphysical) explanation in this context *is*). The result will be explanation either in terms of what makes certain (linguistic) facts true, or in

---

[55] As noted by an anonymous reviewer for this Element, this is a bit (too) fast. What counts as a diagnostic for whether something is fundamental, or for whether something grounds something else? Why exactly aren't those diagnostics sufficient for deciding whether, for example, properties are fundamental such that the diagnostics themselves will give us reasons for and against the claim that properties are fundamental? I agree with the reviewer that a lot remains to be said on this issue. Most of what needs to be said will have to be said somewhere else, but just to give you an idea of what I have in mind, consider what Schaffer has to say in the final section of his 2009 work. Here Schaffer proposes that we "diagnose" what is fundamental as what can serve as a minimally complete supervenience base for everything (else) there is, that we understand it as what has a form that fits all metaphysical possibilities, and that we take it to have a content informed by fundamental physics. As diagnostics for grounding, he suggests that grounding is such that it gives a lot of bang for the buck and that it is such that what is grounded is already latent within that which grounds it. Schaffer thinks that accepting these diagnostics should "make you converge" on the view that there is exactly one fundamental substance that is the whole concrete cosmos (so-called Priority Monism). Suppose he is right. Then it still remains to prove (and I think it will be difficult to prove) that accepting these diagnostics not only gives you reason to but in fact forces you to be a Priority Monist. More important, that reality is structured with the help of grounding relations is compatible with alternative diagnostics of both fundamentality and grounding. Which is why, even if these diagnostics do force us to accept, for example, Priority Monism, "going grounding-theoretical" does not.

terms of what grounds the existence of certain (nonlinguistic) facts. Or something else entirely. Now decide which! What you will then end up with is at least a handful of hypotheses of the following form: if the fact that needs explaining is α, and if explanation (of α) is what we may call β-explanation, then γ will count as an explanation of α. If the fact that needs explaining is α, and if explanation (of α) is what we may call β-explanation, then δ will count as an explanation of α. And so on.

By now you're probably starting to feel a bit tired (doing philosophy – even while sitting in an armchair – has that effect on you!). But you're far from done. Suppose that γ, which β-explains α, is a view on which *properties don't exist.* Suppose that δ, which also β-explains α, is a view on which they *do*. Do properties exist? To find out, γ and δ must be evaluated and compared with respect their theoretical virtue. Or suppose that δ and ε both β-explains α, and that they do so by positing properties. It's just that they view the nature of properties differently (on the δ-view, properties are Platonic Forms, whereas on the ε-view, they are tropes). Are properties Platonic Forms or are they tropes? Again, finding this out requires evaluating and comparing those views with respect to their theoretical virtue.

What will be the result of evaluating and comparing these views with respect to their theoretical virtue? According to Nolan, "[o]nce we know that a theory does as well as, or better than, another on the relevant criteria, we need not be able to rank them on some absolute scale" (2015: 224). According to Nolan, in other words, unless circumstances are exceptional, the outcome will most likely not be a univocal winner followed by a univocal runner-up and so on. Rather, which view does the best relative to the others will depend on which virtue we are for the moment investigating. Add to this the fact that theoretical virtues do not always play nicely together (if a view receives good scores relative to one virtue this may automatically make it score badly on another), it seems that whether properties exist or not is not anything those who go nonlinguistic can determine once and for all.[56]

Is this a point in the approach's disfavor? I don't think so. What going nonlinguistic allows you to do is not nothing. It allows you to see what types of entities *would* account for whatever puzzle you are for the moment engaged in trying to solve. It allows you to see what counts in favor of one view over another, but also what counts against it. It gives you a better understanding of

---

[56] For example, views that score highly when it comes to ontological parsimony (think: one-category ontologies) often require more theory and are hence less theoretically parsimonious (or elegant) than ontologically more expensive views.

the theoretical landscape. I doubt that we can reasonably ask for much more than that.[57]

5 Summary and Conclusions

Suppose you and I seem to be on opposite sides when it comes to whether properties exist: I say that *properties exist*, you say that *they don't*. For my arguments for the existence of properties to have the power to at least in principle persuade you to change your mind, the following needs to be the case: you and I need to agree on what it is we think exists/doesn't exist – that is, we need to agree on what sort of thing it is we are either asserting or denying the existence of- and you and I must also agree on what *would* warrant positing properties (yet disagree about whether or not the need for positing properties is actual, or disagree about whether properties are what best fill this theoretical need). Suppose we *think* we are in agreement about these things, yet we are mistaken. Perhaps this is because we – unbeknownst to us – operate with different ideas about what properties *are*: perhaps I think that properties are whatever so-called nominalizations in true subject-predicate sentences refer to, whereas you think properties must be Platonic Forms, immanent universals, or tropes. Or maybe this is because we – again, unbeknownst to us – have different ideas about the theoretical need properties, if they exist, would have to fill: I might think that what would warrant positing properties would be if properties are needed to account for the meaning and truth of certain sentences, whereas you think that positing properties is warranted only if no other type of posit manages to account for the worldly/experiential fact that many different objects can all have what appears to be the same nature. Or maybe it's for some other reason.

In this Element I have tried to make clear why this situation is not only possible but most likely quite common, and that this is something we must be aware of when engaging in theory evaluation, theory comparison, and theory choice. My original plan was to simply have this Element chart all the ways in which what we assume – about the nature of properties and about how to find

---

[57] The approach is not without its challenges, of course. One such challenge concerns *the point* of comparing theories with respect to virtue. Why think that so doing somehow takes us closer to the truth? Suppose you cannot present any good reason why you think that. Does this mean that going nonlinguistic risks reducing the enterprise of finding out what there is to that of choosing between theories on purely pragmatic grounds? (cf. Morganti and Tahko 2017: 2564 for a good expression of this sort of worry; for some responses, cf., e.g., Paul 2012: 22 and Brenner 2017). Another worry, often voiced by those in favor of "naturalizing" metaphysics (cf., e.g., Ladyman and Ross 2007) is that on this way of conceiving of metaphysics, metaphysics and (natural) science will have the same subject matter, yet science investigates this subject matter so much better (for some pretty convincing objections to this line of reasoning cf., e.g., Paul 2012).

out that properties (fundamentally) exist – may influence if and how different solutions to the problem of properties can be compared and ranked. In the end, though, I did a bit more than that: I argued that although it would be neat if we could conclude – univocally – that properties exist (or not), the nature of metaphysics most likely will not allow us to do that.

References

Allen, S. (2016) *A Critical Introduction to Properties*, Bloomsbury Academic.

Alston, W. (1958) "Ontological Commitments," *Philosophical Studies*, 9(1): 8–17.

Aristotle (1984) *The Complete Works of Aristotle*, vols. 1–2, J. Barnes (ed.), Princeton University Press.

Armstrong, D. M. (1978a) *Nominalism & Realism: Universals & Scientific Realism*, vol. 1, Cambridge University Press.

(1978b) *A Theory of Universals: Universals & Scientific Realism*, vol. 2, Cambridge University Press.

(1980) "Against 'Ostrich' Nominalism: A Reply to Michael Devitt," *Pacific Philosophical Quarterly*, 61(4): 440–449.

(1989) *Universals: An Opinionated Introduction*, Westview Press.

(1997) *A World of States of Affairs*, Cambridge University Press.

(2004) *Truth and Truthmakers*, Cambridge University Press.

Audi, P. (2012) "Grounding: Toward a Theory of the In-Virtue-of Relation," *Journal of Philosophy*, 109(12): 685–711.

(2020) "Why Truthmaking Is Not a Case of Grounding," *Philosophy and Phenomenological Research*, 101(3): 567–590.

Balaguer, M. (2016) "Platonism in Metaphysics," *Stanford Encyclopedia of Philosophy* (Spring 2016 Edition), E. N. Zalta (ed.). https://plato.stanford.edu/archives/spr2016/entries/platonism

Barnes, E. (1994) "Explaining Brute Facts," *PSA: Proceedings of the Biennial Meeting of the Philosophy of Science Association*, 1: 61–68.

Berto F., and D. Nolan (2021) "Hyperintensionality," *Stanford Encyclopedia of Philosophy* (Summer 2021 Edition), E. N. Zalta (ed.). https://plato.stanford.edu/archives/sum2021/entries/hyperintensionality

Bliss, R. (2019) "What Work the Fundamental?" *Erkenntnis*, 84(2): 359–379.

Bliss, R., and K. Trogdon (2021) "Metaphysical Grounding," *Stanford Encyclopedia of Philosophy* (Winter 2021 Edition), E. N. Zalta (ed.). https://plato.stanford.edu/archives/win2016/entries/grounding

Bolander, T. (2017) "Self-Reference," *Stanford Encyclopedia of Philosophy* (Fall 2017 Edition), E. N. Zalta (ed.). https://plato.stanford.edu/archives/fall2017/entries/self-reference

Brenner, A. (2017) "Simplicity As a Criterion of Theory Choice in Metaphysics," *Philosophical Studies*, 174(11): 2687–2707.

Brenner, A., A.-S. Maurin, A. Skiles, R. Stenwall, and N. Thompson (2021) "Metaphysical Explanation," *Stanford Encyclopedia of Philosophy*

(Winter 2021 Edition), E. N. Zalta (ed.). https://plato.stanford.edu/archives/win2021/entries/metaphysical-explanation

Briggs, R. (2012) "Truthmaking without Necessitation," *Synthese*, 189(1): 11–28.

Båve, A. (2015) "A Deflationist Error Theory of Properties," *dialectica*, 69(1): 23–59.

Cameron, R. (2008) "Truthmakers and Ontological Commitment: Or How to Deal with Complex Objects and Mathematical Ontology without Getting into Trouble," *Philosophical Studies*, 140(1): 1–18.

Campbell, K. (1981) "The Metaphysics of Abstract Particulars," *Midwest Studies in Philosophy*, 6(1): 477–488.

(1990) *Abstract Particulars*, Basil Blackwell.

Carnap, R. (1947, enlarged edition 1956) *Meaning and Necessity: A Study in Semantics and Modal Logic*, University of Chicago Press.

Denkel, A. (1996) *Object and Property*, Cambridge University Press.

Devitt, M. (2010[1980]) "'Ostrich' Nominalism or 'Mirage' Realism'?" in *Putting Metaphysics First: Essays on Metaphysics and Epistemology*, Oxford University Press.

Douven, I. (2021) "Abduction," *Stanford Encyclopedia of Philosophy* (Summer 2021 Edition), E. N. Zalta (ed.). https://plato.stanford.edu/archives/sum2021/entries/abduction

Edwards, D. (2014) *Properties*, Polity Press.

Ehring, D. (2011) *Tropes: Properties, Objects, and Mental Causation*, Oxford University Press.

Field, H. (1984) "Platonism for Cheap? Crispin Wright on Frege's Context Principle," *Canadian Journal of Philosophy*, 14: 637–662.

Fine, K. (2012) "Guide to Ground," in *Metaphysical Grounding: Understanding the Structure of Reality*, F. Correia and B. Schnieder (eds.), Cambridge University Press, pp. 37–80.

Giberman, D. (2014) "Tropes in Space," *Philosophical Studies*, 167(2): 453–472.

(online first) "Whole Multiple Location and Universals," *Analytic Philosophy*. https://doi.org/10.1111/phib.12236

Goldstein, L. (1983) "Scientific Scotism: The Emperor's New Trousers or Has Armstrong Made Some Real Strides?" *Australasian Journal of Philosophy*, 61(1): 40–57.

Goodman, N. (1955) *Fact, Fiction, & Forecast*, Harvard University Press.

Guillon, J.-B. (2021) "A Common Sense Defence of Ostrich Nominalism," *Philosophia*, 49: 71–93.

Heil, J. (2003) *From an Ontological Point of View*, Oxford University Press.

Hofweber, T. (2016) *Ontology and the Ambitions of Metaphysics*, Oxford University Press.

Imaguire, G. (2014) "In Defense of Quine's Ostrich Nominalism," *Grazer Philosophische Studien*, 89: 185–203.

(2018) *Priority Nominalism: Grounding Ostrich Nominalism As a Solution to the Problem of Universals*, Springer.

Jago, M. (2006) "Pictures and Nonsense," *Philosophy Now*, 58: 7–9.

Jones, N. (2018) "Nominalist Realism," *Noûs*, 52(4): 808–835.

Keller, J. A. (2017) "Paraphrase and the Symmetry Objection," *Australasian Journal of Philosophy*, 95(2): 365–378.

Küng, G. (1967) *Ontology and the Logistic Analysis of Language*, D. Riedel.

Ladyman, J., and D. Ross (2007) *Every Thing Must Go: Metaphysics Naturalized*, Oxford University Press.

Legg, C. (2001) "Predication and the Problem of Universals," *Philosophical Papers*, 30(2): 117–143.

Lewis, D. (1983) "New Work for a Theory of Universals," *Australasian Journal of Philosophy*, 61(4): 343–377.

(1991) *Parts of Classes*, Wiley-Blackwell.

Macbride, F. (2002) "*The* Problem of Universals and the Limits of Truth-Making," *Philosophical Papers*, 31(1): 27–37.

(2005a) "Ramsey on Universals," in *Ramsey's Legacy*, H. Lillehammer and D. H. Mellor (eds.), Oxford University Press, pp. 83–104.

(2005b) "Negation and Predication: A Defence of Ramsey's Thesis," in *Ramsey's Ontology*, N.-E. Sahlin (ed.), Ontos, pp. 61–87.

(2006) "Predicate Reference," in *The Oxford Handbook of Philosophy of Language*, B. C. Smith (ed.), Oxford University Press, pp. 422–475.

(2021) "Truthmakers," *Stanford Encyclopedia of Philosophy* (Fall 2021 Edition), E. N. Zalta (ed.). https://plato.stanford.edu/archives/fall2021/entries/truthmakers

Markosian, N. (1998) "Brutal Composition," *Philosophical Studies*, 92(3): 211–249.

Maurin, A.-S. (2002) *If Tropes*, Kluwer Academic.

(2005) "Same but Different," *Metaphysica*, 6(1): 129–145.

(2008) "The One over Many," in *Problems from Armstrong*, M. Keinänen and T. De Mey (eds.), Acta Philosophica Fennica.

(2018) "Tropes," *Stanford Encyclopedia of Philosophy* (Summer 2018 Edition), E. N. Zalta (ed.). https://plato.stanford.edu/archives/sum2018/entries/tropes

(2019) "Particulars," *Routledge Encyclopedia of Philosophy*, Taylor and Francis. https://www.rep.routledge.com/articles/thematic/particulars/v-2

(2020) "A Van Inwagean Defense of Constitutionalism," in *Quo Vadis, Metaphysics? Essays in Honor of Peter van Inwagen*, M. Szatkowski (ed.), De Gruyter, pp. 79–93.

McDaniel, K. (2020) *This Is Metaphysics: An Introduction*, Wiley Blackwell.

Mellor, D. H., and A. Oliver (eds.) (1997) *Properties*, Oxford University Press.

Moltmann, F. (2004) "Properties and Kinds of Tropes: New Linguistic Facts and Old Philosophical Insights," *Mind*, 113(449): 1–41.

Moore, G. E. (1925) "A Defense of Common Sense," in *Contemporary British Philosophy*, J. H. Muirhead (ed.), George Allen and Unwin.

Morganti, M., and T. Tahko (2017) "Moderately Naturalistic Metaphysics," *Synthese*, 194(7): 2557–2580.

Mulligan, K., P. Simons, and B. Smith (1984) "Truth-Makers," *Philosophy and Phenomenological Research*, 44(3): 287–321.

Nolan, D. (2015) "The *A Posteriori* Armchair," *Australian Journal of Philosophy*, 93(2): 211–231.

Nozick, R. (1981) *Philosophical Explanations*, Clarendon.

O'Leary-Hawthorne, J., and A. Cortens (1995) "Ontological Nihilism," *Philosophical Studies*, 79(2): 143–165.

Oliver, A. (1996) "The Metaphysics of Properties," *Mind*, 105(417): 1–80.

Orilia, F., and M. Paolini Paoletti (2020) "Properties," *Stanford Encyclopedia of Philosophy* (Winter 2020 Edition), E. N. Zalta (ed.). https://plato .stanford.edu/archives/win2020/entries/properties

Parsons, J. (1999) "There Is No 'Truthmaker' Argument against Nominalism," *Australasian Journal of Philosophy*, 77(3): 325–334.

Paul, L. (2012) "Metaphysics As Modeling: The Handmaiden's Tale," *Philosophical Studies*, 160(1): 1–29.

Peacock, H. (2009) "What's Wrong with Ostrich Nominalism?" *Philosophical Papers*, 38(2): 183–217.

Pickel, B., and N. Mantegani (2012) "A Quinean Critique of Ostrich Nominalism," *Philosophers' Imprint*, 12(6): 1–21.

Plato (1997) *Complete Works*, J. M. Cooper (ed.), Hatchett.

Price, H. (2009) "Metaphysics after Carnap: The Ghost Who Walks?" in *Metametaphysics: New Essays on the Foundations of Ontology*, D. J. Chalmers, D. Manley, and R. Wasserman (eds.), Oxford University Press, pp. 320–346.

Putnam, H. (1987) "Truth and Convention: On Davidson's Refutation of Conceptual Relativism," *dialectica*, 41: 69–77.

Quine, W. V. O. (1948) "On What There Is," *Review of Metaphysics*, 2(5): 21–38.

(1953) "Mr. Strawson on Logical Theory," *Mind*, 62(248): 433–451.

(1960) *Word and Object*, MIT Press.

(1969) *Ontological Relativity and Other Essays*, Columbia University Press.

(1970) *Philosophy of Logic*, Prentice-Hall.

Ramsey, F. P. (1925) "Universals," *Mind*, 34: 401–417.

Reicher, M. (2019) "Nonexistent Objects," *Stanford Encyclopedia of Philosophy* (Winter 2019 Edition), E. N. Zalta (ed.). https://plato.stanford.edu/archives/win2019/entries/nonexistent-objects

Rodriguez-Pereyra, G. (2000) "What Is the Problem of Universals?" *Mind*, 109 (434): 255–273.

(2002) *Resemblance Nominalism: A Solution to the Problem of Universals*, Oxford University Press.

(2019) "Nominalism in Metaphysics," *Stanford Encyclopedia of Philosophy* (Summer 2019 Edition), E. N. Zalta (ed.). https://plato.stanford.edu/archives/sum2019/entries/nominalism-metaphysics

Rosen, G., and J. P. Burgess (2007) "Nominalism Reconsidered," in *The Oxford Handbook of Philosophy of Mathematics and Logic*, S. Shapiro (ed.), Oxford University Press, pp. 515–535.

Russell, B. (1905) "On Denoting," *Mind*, 14(56): 479–493.

(1912) *The Problems of Philosophy*, H. Holt and Company.

Schaffer, J. (2004) "Two Conceptions of Sparse Properties," *Pacific Philosophical Quarterly*, 85: 92–102.

(2008) "Truthmaker Commitments," *Philosophical Studies*, 141(1): 7–19.

(2009) "On What Grounds What," in *Metametaphysics: New Essays on the Foundations of Ontology*, D. J. Chalmers, D. Manley, and R. Wasserman (eds.), Oxford University Press, pp. 347–383.

Schiffer, S. (2003) *The Things We Mean*, Oxford University Press.

Schulte, P. (2019) "Grounding Nominalism," *Pacific Philosophical Quarterly*, 100: 482–505.

Thomasson, A. (2015) *Ontology Made Easy*, Oxford University Press.

Trogdon, K. (2013) "An Introduction to Grounding," in *Varieties of Dependence: Ontological Dependence, Grounding, Supervenience, Response-Dependence*, M. Hoeltje, B. Schnieder, and A. Steinberg (eds.), Philosophia, pp. 97–122.

Van Inwagen, P. (2004) "A Theory of Properties," in *Oxford Studies in Metaphysics*, vol. 1, D. Zimmerman (ed.), Clarendon, pp. 107–138.

(2020) "The Neo-Carnapians," *Synthese*, 197: 7–32.

Varzi, A. (2007) "From Language to Ontology: Beware of the Traps," in *The Categorization of Spatial Entities in Language and Cognition*, M. Aurnague, M. Hickmann, and L. Vieu (eds.), John Benjamin, pp. 269–284.

Williams, D. C. (2018) *The Elements and Patterns of Being*, A. R. J. Fisher (ed.), Oxford University Press.

Wittgenstein, L. (1922) *Tractatus Logico-Philosophicus*, Kegan Paul.

Yablo, S. (2000) "A Paradox of Existence," in *Empty Names, Fiction and the Puzzles of Non-existence*, A. Everett and T. Hofweber (eds.), CSLI Publications, pp. 275–312.

Acknowledgments

I would like to thank all who participated in the discussion of an earlier draft of the first half of this Element when it was presented at a research seminar in theoretical philosophy at the University of Gothenburg (special shoutout to Ylwa Sjölin Wirling). Thanks also to Andrew Brenner and to two anonymous reviewers for Cambridge for very insightful and super-helpful comments and suggestions. I would also like to thank this series' editor, Tuomas Tahko, for inviting me to contribute. Finally, and as always, thank you Johan for your unwavering support in all that matters.

Cambridge Elements

Metaphysics

Tuomas E. Tahko

University of Bristol

Tuomas E. Tahko is Professor of Metaphysics of Science at the University of Bristol, UK. Tahko specializes in contemporary analytic metaphysics, with an emphasis on methodological and epistemic issues: 'meta-metaphysics'. He also works at the interface of metaphysics and philosophy of science: 'metaphysics of science'. Tahko is the author of *Unity of Science* (Cambridge University Press, 2021, *Elements in Philosophy of Science*) and *An Introduction to Metametaphysics* (Cambridge University Press, 2015) and the editor of *Contemporary Aristotelian Metaphysics* (Cambridge University Press, 2012).

About the Series

This highly accessible series of Elements provides brief but comprehensive introductions to the most central topics in metaphysics. Many of the Elements also go into considerable depth, so the series will appeal to both students and academics. Some Elements bridge the gaps between metaphysics, philosophy of science, and epistemology.

Printed in the United States
by Baker & Taylor Publisher Services